Amp Up
Your Sales

Amp Up
Your Sales

Powerful Strategies That
Move Customers to Make
Fast, Favorable Decisions

ANDY PAUL

AMACOM AMERICAN MANAGEMENT ASSOCIATION

New York • Atlanta • Brussels • Chicago • Mexico City
San Francisco • Shanghai • Tokyo • Toronto • Washington, D.C.

Bulk discounts available. For details visit:
www.amacombooks.org/go/specialsales
Or contact special sales:
Phone: 800-250-5308 / Email: specialsls@amanet.org
View all the AMACOM titles at: www.amacombooks.org
American Management Association: www.amanet.org

This publication is designed to provide accurate and authoritative information in regard to the subject matter covered. It is sold with the understanding that the publisher is not engaged in rendering legal, accounting, or other professional service. If legal advice or other expert assistance is required, the services of a competent professional person should be sought.

Library of Congress Cataloging-in-Publication Data

Paul, Andy.
Amp up your sales : powerful strategies that move customers to make fast, favorable decisions / Andy Paul.
    pages cm
Includes bibliographical references and index.
ISBN 978-0-8144-3487-1 (pbk.) — ISBN 0-8144-3487-8 (pbk.) — ISBN 978-0-8144-3488-8 (ebook) 1. Selling. 2. Sales management. I. Title.
HF5438.25.P376 2015
658.85—dc23

                                                                      2014024013

About AMA

American Management Association (www.amanet.org) is a world leader in talent development, advancing the skills of individuals to drive business success. Our mission is to support the goals of individuals and organizations through a complete range of products and services, including classroom and virtual seminars, webcasts, webinars, podcasts, conferences, corporate and government solutions, business books, and research. AMA's approach to improving performance combines experiential learning—learning through doing—with opportunities for ongoing professional growth at every step of one's career journey.

Printing number
10 9 8 7 6 5 4 3 2 1

Contents

Foreword

"It's not what you sell. It's how you sell."

Let's take a quick look at where we are. Three societal and technological changes over the past few decades have totally disrupted business and irrevocably changed selling.

Globalization, a force that's been occurring for thousands of years, has made the world a smaller place—and it's brought new, competitive entrants from just about everywhere. Your marketplace is now crowded. You look a lot like your competitors, and they look a lot like you.

The Internet has disintermediated whole industries, like book sales (think Amazon.com), television (think Netflix, Hulu, and YouTube), and newspapers. If a salesperson can't add value to a buying decision, that purchase can be made via a quick and easy transaction over the Web.

The final change affecting the sales force is commoditization. In the 1970s and 1980s, we were able to speak about a sustainable competitive advantage—the ability to do something in a way that was so difficult to duplicate that you could dominate your market for decades. The idea of "sustainable" is now quaint. What you sell, no matter how good, is going to be copied—and with lightning speed.

But there's good news. Because it matters more how you sell than what you sell, you're empowered to act in a way that provides you with a massive competitive advantage—and one not easily duplicated. There's a way you can "Amp Up Your Sales."

By learning what it really means to buy and to sell, you'll discover the advantage gained by providing your customers with the help they need to make buying decisions (ones favorable to you). Once you understand the mechanics of selling this way, you're ready for a move that will differentiate and define you in the minds of your prospects and clients.

If you want to compress your sales cycle, win new clients faster, and help them realize the advantages of what you sell sooner, you need to be more than responsive. You need to be super-responsive. In a short, powerful section of this book, you'll recognize that helping your clients make a decision means giving them the information they need now. And not a minute later.

Creating a competitive advantage means creating more value than your competitors do. This means more than creating value through your solution. Remember, it's *how* you sell that matters. Your time-starved clients expect you to create the maximum value during every interaction.

Selling is more challenging than it's ever been. If you're a salesperson, the book you hold in your hands holds the answers to the challenges you face. If you're a sales manager or sales leader, it's a powerful toolkit that can fundamentally change *how* your sales force engages your prospects in clients. You need a strategic plan to produce better results, and you need the tactics that allow you to execute and win. You'll find both in *Amp Up Your Sales.*

S. Anthony Iannarino
www.thesalesblog.com
Westerville, Ohio

Introduction

SALES IS ONE of the few professions where nearly everyone is searching for the edge that will make him or her better. It doesn't matter if you're the top salesperson at your company or are simply working hard to reach the next level of productivity. The desire to constantly improve is the same.

In that sense, salespeople are like professional athletes whose careers and incomes depend on achieving and maintaining a level of uncommon excellence. Athletes incorporate the latest knowledge about diet, fitness, strength, and mental focus into their training regimens in order to achieve even small increments in the improvement in their performance. After all, in most sports, a 1 percent improvement can be the difference between winning and losing—between being the champion or an also-ran.

So it is in sales. You only have to be 1 percent better than your competitors to win your customer's business. However, there's a catch. *You* have to generate that 1 percent margin of victory. Why? We live and work in a global economy where the pace of technological innovation has lowered the barriers to entry to most market segments, resulting in an explosion in the number of products and services competing for the attention of the customer. As more of these products and services enter a market, the differences between them, both real and perceived, narrow. The result is that in the eyes of the customer, all competitive products and services look increasingly alike. This means that the responsibility for creating the meaningful differentiation between you and your competitors, that 1 percent difference, the margin between winning an order or losing it, falls squarely upon your shoulders.

In my previous book, *Zero-Time Selling*, I wrote that in this modern global economy, *how* you sell is more important than *what* you sell (and I provided ten strategies for companies to use to differentiate themselves based on how they sell). I believe this statement is truer today than when I first wrote it. Now the challenge becomes how to effectively compete in this changing business environment. How can you break through the noise to attract and retain the attention of busy and distracted customers? How can you maximize the value of your selling to help your customers achieve their objectives? In short, how can you amp up your selling to stand out in a crowd of undifferentiated competitors? I wrote this book to provide the answers to these questions and more.

As I speak to audiences of salespeople around the country, the question I'm most frequently asked is, "What's the best sales process or sales methodology that I can use?" My response is that the best sales process is the one that works for you. Companies necessarily have their own particular sales procedures that they want salespeople to follow. But the fact remains that when salespeople interact with a customer, they'll fall back on a personalized selling process that they believe works for them. This will never change. Salespeople will always adapt corporate sales procedures or given selling methodologies to an individual selling process that fits into their comfort zone. And there's nothing wrong with that—if it works.

The problem is that for too many salespeople, their comfort zone doesn't align with the buying and decision-making requirements of the customer. Industry studies show that year after year, fewer than 50 percent of salespeople achieve their quotas. Some of this shortfall could be written off as "grading on a curve." But I believe that the trouble is more fundamental than that. My experience has shown me that most salespeople lack an unambiguous understanding of what they need to do each and every time they interact with a customer. Selling is an interactive process. It's not something that you do *to* your prospects and customers. It's a process that you undertake in collaboration *with* them to help achieve a specific objective.

Amp Up Your Sales revolves around three main themes: (1) simplifying your selling, (2) maximizing the value of your selling, and (3) amplifying your sales responsiveness.

At the beginning of my sales career, one of my first sales managers assured me, "Selling is simple. It's not easy. But it is simple."

Well, sales should be simple. But usually it isn't.

In Part I of this book, I introduce you to the core concepts of selling (and buying) that all salespeople must understand in order to simplify their selling. I break core sales concepts—like selling, buying, time, and decision making—down to their smallest levels. In physics, this is called reducing complex problems to first principles. I'll use what I call the first principles of sales to illustrate what selling and buying really mean in today's modern sales environment.

You may be tempted to skim over this section. Don't. You probably think you understand what selling is. But, as you'll learn in Chapter 1, it's not what you think. If you're going to invest your time in taking steps to become a superior salesperson, then it's essential that you first develop a clear understanding of what it means to sell. After all, how can you improve your sales skills if you don't know what the goal should be? How can you improve your aim if you can't clearly see the target?

Similarly, you may think you know what buying is. You may believe that you understand how customers decide to give you their time. Or that you know how every customer falls into one of two types of decision makers and how this categorization affects every sales opportunity. Or that you know which factors influence the customer's first perception of you and how this can win or lose the sale for you. Or that you know how to win the sale before winning the order. But chances are that this will be new for you.

How will this knowledge simplify your selling? If you really understand what selling and buying are, especially from the perspective of your customers, then this helps you focus on just those sales actions that move the needle, that deliver maximum value to customers, and that help them make favorable purchasing decisions quickly and with the smallest investment of their time and money possible.

In Part II, we'll focus on responsiveness, the single most important sales skill that you must master and integrate into your selling. You don't have to master many skills in order to be proficient at your job. You don't need to be the smoothest cold caller, the most polished presenter, or the most knowledgeable about your products to win some orders. But if you're not completely responsive to your customers, you'll never reach the sales goals that you've set for yourself.

In Part III, the focus is on how you can maximize the value you deliver to the customer through your selling. I'll open your eyes to a new way of visualizing value as a core attribute of your selling. As a result, you will be prepared to deliver the maximum value each and every time you interact with your customers (irrespective of the method that you're employing—phone, e-mail, social, text, video, or in-person calls). This leads to accelerated trust-building and compressed customer decision-making cycles. You'll learn how to eliminate the valueless sales calls and wasted selling time that plague so many salespeople and inhibit their productivity.

In Parts IV–VIII of the book, I'll use these building blocks to provide simple, easily implemented sales strategies that create tangible sales differentiation and that will help make your selling memorable to the customer. It doesn't matter what type of product or service you sell, and it doesn't matter how costly or inexpensive the product is. The goal on the part of your prospects is the same: They're looking for your support to help them make an informed purchase decision. Deliver value to help the customer quickly move through the buying process, and you'll create the building blocks of a relationship that will make it easier for the customer to choose you.

As you will learn, what makes selling simple is that a relatively small number of sales processes, when mastered and applied in a consistent and disciplined manner, will enable you to accelerate trust, deliver maximum value, tangibly differentiate you from your competitors, and empower your customers to make fast and favorable decisions.

Most important, all the sales processes and strategies discussed in this book are under your direct control. You can't control your customers and the actions they take. You can control only what you do. But if you take the right steps at the right time, you'll move your customers to make the timely buying decisions that will amp up your sales.

Everyone can achieve uncommon excellence in sales. Especially you.

PART I

Simplifying Your Selling

CHAPTER 1

What Is Selling?

THE MOST PRECISE definition of selling I've ever seen is from Jeff Bezos, Amazon's founder and CEO. In an interview with the *Harvard Business Review* (January–February 2013), Bezos said, "We don't make money when we sell things. We make money when we help customers make a purchase decision."

What is your role as a seller? To be more precise, what is your primary role as a salesperson in relation to your prospects and customers? Every day, when you're confronted with the importance of effectively interacting with your customers, what mental image do you have of the primary task you're supposed to be accomplishing? Are you conscious of the role you're playing in the overall sales process?

Here's the central challenge for salespeople today: You operate in a fast-paced, information-driven, crazy-busy, increasingly competitive and interconnected economy. As a result, you have fewer opportunities to meaningfully engage with your prospects and customers before they make their purchase decisions. This means you have to be more prepared than ever to provide maximum value to your prospects during each precious interaction in the selling/buying process.

Understanding selling is one of the core building blocks to increasing your sales performance. It would be so easy to lightly skip past this step and say to yourself:

"Of course, I know what selling is."

Really? What is selling?

"Giving something to someone in exchange for money."

Giving what?

"A product. Or a service."

Why are you giving this to them?

"Because they asked for it."

They just asked for your product or service, with no other questions?

"Well, sure, they had lots of questions."

And . . .?

"Lots of questions. Way too many questions."

Did you answer their questions?

"Of course we did."

Did you get their order?

"Of course we did."

Could you have won the order without answering your customer's questions?

"No."

So what is selling?

At its most fundamental level, selling is simply an exchange of information between the buyer and you, the seller. Selling is the process by which customers provide you with information about their requirements, and, in return, you provide them the necessary and relevant information about your products and services that enables them to make a buying decision. The key to consistent sales success resides in the process you execute to gather and provide the necessary information the prospect requires to make a decision.

The simplest way for you to understand the nature of selling is to remember that it has only two parts: questions and answers. Your customer has requirements and questions. Selling is *how* you ask your questions and *how* you provide the answers to your customer's questions. Those questions and answers will have the most decisive impact on your ability to win the customer's business.

If you noticed, I highlighted the word *how* in the last paragraph. In fact, I am highlighting *how* throughout the rest of this chapter to make certain that you clearly grasp and internalize this most important point about selling:

How you sell is more important than what you sell.

How you provide information to your customers to help them make a decision will be a more decisive factor in winning the business than your product's features and benefits.

Here's why: In a world where the unending cycle of technological innovation and rapid globalization have dramatically reduced the barriers to entry into new markets, it's little surprise that the number of competitors in nearly every category of product and service has exploded over the past 10 to 15 years. Combined with the growth and power of the Internet that provides an often bewildering trove of information about all the competitors to interested prospects, it's little wonder that, in the eyes of buyers, all suppliers seeking their business begin to look alike. The challenge for you is to create meaningful differentiation that enables you to stand apart from your competitors and to make it easier and faster for your prospects to make informed purchase decisions.

You'll want to highlight the following sentence with a yellow marker so that you can come back and review it time and again: *Sustainable, repeatable sales success is less about what you sell and more about* how *you sell.* In this case, *how* is not about style but about substance: *how* you follow up sales leads, *how* you ask the questions that define the customer's requirements, *how* responsive you are to customer requests, *how* quickly and completely you provide information and answers to your prospects.

This means that you have to maintain a laser focus on *how* you can be completely responsive to a prospect or customer's requirements for information. A standard question salespeople are told to ask themselves is, "What am I doing right now that is getting me closer to an order?" On the surface it would seem to be a good question to ask. It puts the focus on the now and places the priority on action. Unfortunately, it's also completely backward. It has the focus on the order rather than on the customer. One is the cart. The other is the horse. It's important that you understand which is which.

If the primary method by which you can differentiate yourself, your offering, and your company is *how* you provide the value and information that supports your customer's efforts to make a purchase decision, then the order will follow. An order is merely the outcome of selling, not the act of selling itself. Therefore, the most important question all salespeople should be asking themselves is, "What am I doing right now that is helping my customer to make a purchase decision?"

I call this necessary focus on *how* you sell the good news/bad news conundrum. Let's start with the good news: Your success in selling today is primarily based on *how* you sell, not what you sell. Just think how liberating that is for you. When your ultimate success in sales is based on *how* you sell, it means that all the tools you need to win are under your direct control. Now it's up to you *how* you provide the information that helps your customers make a purchase decision, from the moment you respond to a new lead to the moment you receive an order. This focus on *how* eliminates nearly all the external dependencies that hampered your selling in the past. This is not just good news. This is great news!

Now the bad news: Your success in selling today is primarily based on *how* you sell, not what you sell. That sounds just like the good news, right? As I've mentioned, when the products and services of all sellers increasingly look alike to customers, *how* you sell is more important than what you sell. This puts you into what I call the No Excuses Sales Zone. If your success depends on *how* you sell, and the *how* of *how* you sell is completely under your control, then you have no excuses for not achieving your sales goals. You can't point the finger at the lack of this feature or that benefit and say that it's holding you back. The *how* is up to you, and you have no excuses for not using it to your competitive advantage.

I've worked with thousands of salespeople over the decades of my career. Almost every one of them was sincere in their desire to become successful in all phases of their chosen profession. Yet nearly all of them lacked a clear vision and detailed understanding of what their sales role entailed. By understanding what selling really is, as well as the importance of *how*, you possess the foundation to build the skills necessary to take your sales to the next level.

CHAPTER 2

Understanding Your Selling Process

THE MOST FUNDAMENTAL problem in sales is that salespeople truly don't understand the purpose of what they're doing each day they are working the phones and their e-mail to develop new business. If you haven't internalized what selling is at a macro level, then your ability to formulate relevant and effective sales strategies that swiftly move a prospect through the buying cycle is compromised.

Salespeople are not to blame. They've probably been misled by their CEO and sales managers into thinking that sales is all about taking orders—which would be the right answer to the question if it weren't so wrong.

Rex Ryan, coach of the NFL's New York Jets, is considered a leading innovator in the development of defensive formations and schemes to contain the high-octane offenses that dominate in the league. When asked about his players' success in responding in real time to the numerous variables that offenses throw at them on each play, he said, "It's all about concepts. If you teach the concepts well, the players will understand it. Once they know the concepts, then it is easy for them to execute."

If you're going to invest your time in taking steps to become a superior salesperson, then it's essential that you first develop a clear and unambiguous understanding of the concepts of what it means to sell. After all, how can you improve your sales skills if you don't know what the goal should be? How can you improve your aim if you can't clearly see the target?

Selling is a process. It's frequently compared to a manufacturing process in which a prescribed sequence of steps must be executed to obtain the desired end product: an order. But is selling really a process that can be compared to a production line in a factory? Not really. The problem is that a focus on the "sales process" is nearly always on the output of that process and not on the quality of its inputs.

So, yes, selling definitely is a process. But instead of thinking about it as an industrial mechanical process, it's more useful for you to think of it as a recipe.

Every recipe has two parts: the ingredients and the preparation. As any chef will tell you, the success of an entrée or pastry begins and ends with the quality of the ingredients. Neither the chefs' preparations nor the finely honed cooking skills that comprise their process can compensate for poor ingredients. The same holds true for missing ingredients. If I tried to make chocolate chip cookies without the chocolate chips, I would just have . . . cookies.

Let's consider your recipe for selling. Instead of thinking of ingredients and preparation, think about concepts and process. You can have what you feel is a robust sales process, but if you don't incorporate the right sales concepts into your selling, then your chances of success are diminished. Like the chocolate chip cookies without the chocolate chips, your selling will lack the ingredients necessary to move your customers to buy from you.

What are the required ingredients of a sales process? Imagine that this entire book is a recipe for your favorite energy drink. In this case, it's specifically a sales energy drink. In the first two parts of this book, I'll give you the ingredients for making your own sales energy drink—the sales concepts that will energize, amplify, and maximize your personal sales productivity.

The remaining parts of the book are focused on how you will blend these new sales ingredients into a responsive, trusted, and accelerated selling process that produces consistently great results.

Productivity consultant David Allen is the master of getting things done. In fact, his best-selling book, *Getting Things Done*, is about time management. However, many of the lessons he teaches in his book apply to selling as well. The most relevant lesson for salespeople involves how to break down a bigger task (i.e., getting an order) into the logical sequence of events required to help the customer make a purchase decision. Allen talks about needing to know at each step of your process the "very next physical action required to move the situation forward." In selling terms, this means knowing at each step of your sales process the very next physical action required to move the customer one step closer to making a purchase decision.

This is where salespeople often trip up. The problem is that you really don't know the "very next physical action required to move the situation forward." Oh sure, you'll say to yourself that you need to send a follow-up e-mail to the customer. But why are you sending that e-mail? What information are you going to provide that will move the customer's buying cycle forward? What's the "next physical action" that you want the customer to take in response to your e-mail?

Let me give you an example of what this means. We all know how to change a lightbulb in a ceiling fixture at home, but have you ever given any thought as to how many steps there are in that process? I researched the answer online and found one website with an illustrated guide to changing lightbulbs (I'm not kidding). It showed that the process could be accomplished in four easy steps:

1. Turn off the light.

2. Stand on a ladder.

3. Replace the old bulb.

4. Turn on the light to test that the bulb is working.

But Allen shows that the list is incomplete. There are many more steps in this process. What's missing are the "very next physical actions" required to move the process of changing a lightbulb forward. For instance, after you turn off the light, the ladder doesn't magically materialize inside your house. You have to go out to the garage, get your ladder, and bring it inside. Once you have incorporated all the "very next physical actions" into this process, you suddenly have a realistic picture of the work required to replace a lightbulb. Four steps become 14.

1. Turn off the light.

2. Go to the garage and bring your ladder inside.

3. Set up the ladder beneath the light.

4. Stand on the ladder.

5. Check the wattage of the burned-out bulb.

7. Go to the garage and find the appropriate wattage lightbulb.

8. Stand on the ladder.

9. Unscrew the burned-out bulb.

10. Screw in the new bulb.

12. Turn on the light to test the new bulb.

13. Dispose of the old bulb.

14. Return the ladder to the garage.

Now let's apply this concept to your selling. This is how salespeople look at their selling process:

1. Respond to a sales lead.

2. Do a discovery call.

3. Do a demonstration.

4. Send a quote.

5. Close the order.

Unfortunately, this overly simplistic view of selling doesn't reflect the "very next physical actions" required to move the process forward.

Let's take a closer look at just one step: "Respond to a sales lead." Is this really just a single step in your selling process? What happens when I start applying the concept of the "very next physical action" to this single task? Suddenly it begins blossoming to look like this:

1. Receive the sales lead via e-mail.

2. Visit the prospect's website.

3. Read about the prospect's product and service offerings.

4. Read about the prospect's management team.

5. Read about the prospect's company history.

6. Browse through the prospect company's blog.

7. Do a Google search for the prospect company.

8. Read the latest news about the prospect company.

Hold it there. I'm going to stop at step number eight. There are actually 24 smaller actions in total that make up "Respond to a sales lead." Twenty-four! (If you want to learn the other 16 "very next physical actions" required to respond to a sales lead, then visit my website at http://www.zerotimeselling.com/respond-to-a-lead/.) And you can't skip any of these steps if you expect to win the order.

Sadly, all too often salespeople do skip essential steps in their selling process. If just one element of a sales process breaks down into 24 smaller but necessary steps, then how many crucial steps, in total, are you over-looking in your own selling process?

In my business, I work with a great many salespeople. Both those who are above quota and those working hard to meet it face the same problem: an incomplete understanding of the physical actions required for each and every prospect each and every day. Why does one step lead to another? What is the logic that makes all the steps of their selling process work together?

By the time you finish reading this book, you'll have a complete understanding of the detailed ingredients of your selling process, which are the driving concepts and logic behind the physical actions required at each step as you move your customer closer to making a decision.

CHAPTER 3

Balancing Selling and Buying

THIS IS NOT a trick question: Are you selling, or is your customer buying?

The answer is both. On every deal that you work, both a sales cycle and buying cycle(s) are occurring. Understanding the balance between the two is essential for every seller.

Let's start at the beginning. What is buying? Buying is simply an organized search by a prospect for the specific information she needs to make an informed purchase decision to buy the right product(s) to fit her needs. The customer gathers that information in the form of answers to the questions she asks you. How a seller conveys that information to the prospect will be the difference between getting an order and losing a customer.

So buying, like selling (see Chapter 1), is really about two things: questions and answers. Your customer asks questions, and you have answers. It's how you provide the answers that will be decisive in your ability to win the business. And as I'll show you in Chapter 10, the first seller with the answers wins.

As mentioned, in every sales opportunity there is both a sales cycle and at least one buying cycle. There are two essential points for you to remember about this:

1. A seller cannot control the customer's buying process. The customer is in charge of their buying cycle. Despite the hundreds of

books and articles published by sales authors who purport to teach you the importance of controlling your prospect, it can't be done. You can only hope to influence it.

2. The only way you can influence the course of the customer's buying cycle is through the one thing over which you have complete control: your selling process and how you sell.

Why is this so important to you? Because the sole purpose of a sales process is to support the buying cycle by helping the customer accomplish a single task: making a fully informed decision to purchase the right product or service. If you, as a seller can also, at the same time, shape how you sell to enable the customer to make that purchase decision in the shortest time possible, then you will have created value for the buyer, established credibility, built trust, differentiated your offer and your company, and put yourself at the head of the pack competing for the business.

The balance of power has shifted to the customer. In the pre-Internet world, the buyers—your prospects—were almost completely dependent on sellers for information about the products and services they wanted to buy. When I began my sales career for a big computer company (both the computers and the company were big), there were no websites to search and very few reliable third-party sources of information about products that a customer could use to guide and shape a purchase decision. My customers had one source of information about the products and services I was selling: me. In those days, customers could buy only as fast as salespeople were prepared to sell to them. The result was a much more casually paced buying cycle because customers had few options to control the speed of the process.

Then, to the initial consternation of buyer and seller alike, the Internet upended that whole arrangement. However, buyers quickly realized that the Internet could be a tool that reshaped how they evaluated products for purchase. Within a matter of years, the customer was no longer dependent on the seller for product information. Brochures were replaced with websites that were usually full of more information than even the salesperson could provide. Buyers suddenly had access to a whole spectrum of information that hadn't existed before or that had been shielded from them by the sellers. Online communities provided users with forums where they could voice their unvarnished opinions about products and services to all who were interested. Now customers were in charge of the buying process.

This information explosion has taken from the sellers' hands what little control of the buying process they had. No longer are customers waiting for you to sell to them. In fact, as I'll discuss in Chapter 11, your customers will have moved through a substantial portion of their buying process before they first speak with you, and when they do, you'll have to be prepared to sell to them in a different fashion.

Here are a couple of key points to remember about buying cycles:

- *Your prospect will have a separate buying process for every seller she is talking to in a competitive deal.* As important as understanding what buying is, as a seller you need to be aware that more than one buying cycle will be occurring simultaneously on every sales opportunity. Again, your prospect will have a separate buying process for every seller in a competitive deal. Even if you believe that you are the only supplier bidding for a customer's business, you have to assume that your prospect is evaluating the value of your offer against the value of making no decision and doing nothing. In that case, doing nothing is your competition—and it has a buying cycle too.

- *Each buying cycle moves at a pace that is all its own.* If you can respond more quickly and completely to your prospect's information requirements, then their buying cycle for your product may move forward more rapidly than it would for your competitors. How efficiently and effectively you provide information and answers to your prospect can be the difference between getting an order and losing a customer. If you, as a seller, empower your prospect to make a purchase decision with the least investment of time possible, in order to move more rapidly through the buying cycle, then you'll successfully create real value for the buyer, lay the foundation for a trust-based relationship, and truly differentiate yourself from your competitors.

Successful salespeople are those who can most closely align their selling resources (product knowledge and industry expertise) with the customers' buying needs (information requirements) to enable them to make the optimum informed decision in the least time possible.

CHAPTER 4

The Mechanics of Decision Making

IN THE FIRST two chapters, we examined what selling really is, how you need to think about your selling process relative to the needs of your customer, and the primary motivation that drives the customer's buying process.

Now let's focus on some of the fundamental mechanics of customer decision making. Actually, there's no reason to qualify it here by calling it "customer" decision making, because whether one is buying a car or deciding where to meet friends for dinner, the decision-making process is roughly the same.

We are all decision makers. As you read through this chapter, take a moment to think about how its lessons apply to you as well as to your selling. If you develop greater self-insight into how you make decisions, it will help you to become more sensitive and more attuned to the process your customers have to go through to make their decisions—which will increase the odds of positive outcomes for you.

As early as possible in your sales process with a customer, you need to understand whom you are selling to. This may sound a bit obvious. But I'm not referring to "whom" in the sense of a job title. I would expect you to know that the decision maker is the owner, CEO, vice president of ops, or engineering manager.

When I ask "whom" you are selling to, I want you to tell me which type of decision maker you are interacting with. It can make a significant difference in how you sell if you know to "whom" you are selling.

Let me explain. Every one of your customers falls into one of two broad categories of decision maker: a satisficer (pronounced "sa-tis-fys-er") or a maximizer. I did not make that up! Herbert Simon, the Nobel Prize–winning economist from Carnegie Mellon, first coined these terms based on research he conducted back in the 1950s.

You need to understand which type of decision maker your prospects are because it influences how you're going to sell to them—or whether you'll even choose to sell to them. You also need to understand which category of decision maker you fall into because this can influence how you sell.

Satisficers make a decision or take action once their basic decision criteria are met. Satisficers are people who make the classic good-enough decision. They are prospects who will buy from the first seller who satisfactorily provides the information they need to make a purchase decision.

Satisficers will make their decision once they've gathered a certain minimum amount of information because in their minds there's not a big enough ROI to justify the investment of additional time or effort to keep researching their options. Satisficers make decisions and don't look back. Typically they experience less buyer's remorse because they don't stress about whether they've made the absolutely best decision. They made the decision that was good enough to meet their requirements and to achieve their objectives.

Maximizers are decision makers who can't make a decision until they've examined every possible alternative and are convinced that they've made the best possible choice. Research shows that maximizers do indeed make the best decisions. Somewhat ironically, but not unexpectedly, they are also more likely to be unhappy with their decision than a satisficer. Why? Because maximizers always worry that they may have overlooked something, that there was some better option that they neglected to consider.

Now let's do a quick exercise to find out if you are a satisficer or maximizer. I'd like you to think back to the last car you purchased or leased.

After you conducted your initial research online, how many dealerships did you visit before you made your purchase/lease decision?

One or two dealerships? Good work! You are a satisficer. You decided that the marginal return on the investment of additional hours of your time to visit yet another dealer just wasn't worth it. The information you had already gathered was good enough to feel comfortable making your decision.

Three or more dealerships? I hesitate to label you, but you're probably a maximizer. You can be comforted by the fact that at the end of the day you likely bought a car that met all of your decision criteria. The trade-off was that you spent a lot more of your limited time searching for the best possible car for your needs. And I suspect you probably woke up in the middle of the night to kick yourself for not waiting a few months to see what next year's model offered.

A 2012 National Automobile Dealers Association survey found that the average car buyer visited 1.2 dealers prior to making a purchase decision. We can safely extrapolate from this information that most people tend to fall more on the satisficer end of the spectrum than on the maximizer end. (We rarely are all one type or the other. People can be satisficers for some decisions and maximizers for others.)

So when you look at this in terms of your customer mix—and I'll teach more about buyer qualification later in the book—you have to keep in mind that every buyer you work with will fall into one of these two categories. You need to determine which type you are working with in the early stages of your qualification process.

How are you supposed to determine which category they're in? Just ask them. For instance, ask about a previous decision they've made. If you're talking to them about selling a replacement to an existing product, then ask the decision maker about the decision-making process they went through on the original purchase (the number of vendors they talked to, their internal process, and the length of the decision cycle). That will give you a strong indication of which type of decision maker you are dealing with.

This knowledge of your customer should have an impact on your selling. The satisficer will be open to making a faster decision. If you can be responsive (see Chapter 10 for a full description of responsiveness) to satisficers and quickly provide them the information that meets their minimum requirements for making a purchase decision, then you can dramatically increase your chances of winning their business. In dealing with a satisficer, the speed of your selling is very important.

The speed of your selling is critical to maximizers as well. Maximizers may want to evaluate every alternative that exists, but the fact is that they don't have any more time than satisficers to complete their buying process. The keys for selling to these decision makers are immediate responsiveness and proactive transparency. One difficulty in selling to maximizers is that they evaluate so many different options that they may have a hard time remembering you. This means you have to create clear differentiation by quickly and completely responding to a maximizer's need for specific information. This will make your selling memorable.

Another way to help a maximizer move more quickly through the buying process is what I call *proactive transparency.* For instance, if you have six competitors on a deal, create a complete, unbiased competitive matrix featuring all six of their products (as well as your own) and present it to the prospect. This is a trust builder, a differentiator, and potentially a memorable time saver for the prospect.

By contrast, depending on the nature of the business you are in and the products you offer, you may want to steer clear of maximizers. If you have a quick-turn product, something that typically sells after just one or two sales calls, then you should consider whether you would be better off letting your competitors spend their limited time selling to the maximizers.

Lastly, examine how your own buying behavior affects your selling. If you're a maximizer, for instance, then you'll need to be very careful about selling to another maximizer. One of my clients is a company that sells a technical product to customers in the Silicon Valley area, many of whom, as you might expect, are detailed-oriented engineers with maximizer tendencies. One of the client's salespeople, Earl, was himself a maximizer. Earl reveled in long, detailed discussions with his customers about the technical attributes of his products. Naturally, he attracted maximizer customers. The result was that Earl didn't have the time to support more than just a few prospects, and the length of time they took to make their decision was more than double the time that satisficer prospects required with other salespeople. Needless to say, Earl wasn't making his number.

There's a lot of research on the mental process people go through to make a decision to buy something. Let me boil it down to five key points that you must keep in mind as you formulate your sales strategies:

1. When people make a decision, they follow a process with a certain number of steps. Marketing people like to talk about four steps in the decision-making process using the acronym AIDA: awareness, interest, desire, action. IBM used to train their sales team in The 5-Call Close.

2. People move sequentially through the steps of their decision-making process. Imagine that you are in the Olympics, competing in the men's 110-meter hurdles. As you lower yourself into the starting blocks, you look down the straightaway of the track and see stretched out before you ten hurdles that you need to clear before you reach the finish line. If you want to win the race, you have to leap over each hurdle in order. You can't decide to hurdle only the even-numbered barriers and then go back for the odd-numbered ones.

2. Decision makers don't skip a step in their process. You are back in the Olympic hurdle competition again. You can't decide to skip hurdle number seven and still win the competition. There are no shortcuts in the decision-making process.

3. Each step in the decision-making process is associated with certain information requirements. This means that each step of the process contains questions that need to be answered.

4. Customers will not move from the current step in their decision-making process to the next until their questions have been answered.

These rules apply to satisficers and maximizers alike. However, there will be differences in how they apply them. Satisficers may have fewer steps in their decision-making process and will likely have fewer questions that need to be answered at each step. Maximizers may require more detailed information before feeling comfortable moving to the next step in their process. As I stressed earlier, be sure to identify the decision-maker type early in your qualification.

Let's look at how some of these points apply to your selling. Think back to a sales situation with a good prospect when the sales cycles suddenly and unexpectedly became flabby and stretched out. When a sales cycle slows or veers off course, a salesperson's first tendency is to point the finger of blame at the buyer. After all, isn't it always the customer who's the culprit when the sales cycle stalls? No. In fact, the opposite is true. When the buyer stops making progress toward closing an order, it's nearly always the seller's fault. Why?

If you aren't providing your prospect with the information she needs to move on to the subsequent step in her decision-making process, then the buying cycle will screech to a halt. If the deal you're working on suddenly loses momentum, before you begin pointing a finger at the customer, take a look in the mirror. You need to quickly engage with the customer to determine what's needed from you to satisfy the information requirements for the current step of the buying cycle and to get your sales cycle back on track.

Let's say that you're working on a sales opportunity that has just one competitor. Suddenly the deal slows down, and you're stuck on step two. The customer is waiting for you to respond to a question you were asked in an e-mail two days ago. The customer needs to consider your response before moving on to the next step. Unfortunately for you, your competitor didn't miss a beat, quickly answering the question on the very day it was received. Now your very good, very qualified prospect is working on step three of the evaluation and decision-making process with your competitor while you're spinning your wheels on step two (and you probably haven't even asked the customer why). Ouch! Don't let that happen to you.

CHAPTER 5

The Ratio of Planning to Action

SALES IS A profession for people who like to think. If you want a job that requires you to do the same thing day after day, then you should find another line of work. Like working on an assembly line.

Even though selling is a process, I've often witnessed managers who take the sales-is-just-an-assembly-line school of thought a few steps too far. They believe that if you plug any individual into a well-conceived process, that person can achieve a basic level of sales success. While I'm a great believer in the power of a process in selling and will discuss the importance of the sales process in later chapters, the addition of even a modicum of creative thinking or creative initiative in any sales situation will always spell the difference between average achievement and outstanding performance.

Selling is an interactive process between you and a buyer. As I'll discuss in Part III, "Maximizing Value," each interaction with a customer demands a level of analysis and planning beyond what you might normally expect. This means that you've got to guard against being a reactive seller. A reactive seller operates purely by the book. "If the customer does A, then I'll do B." The problem is that every prospect and customer who enters into a buying process with you is unique. No two are alike in their needs, their personalities, their business perspectives, the methods in which they gather and analyze information, or the steps they take in making their decisions.

Think instead about being an interactive seller. First and foremost, an interactive seller is a thinker whose actions are influenced by the customer's actions. Instead of using the reactive "If the customer does A, then I'll do B" approach, the interactive seller says, "If the customer does A, then I need to analyze why he did A, evaluate the range of potential responses (B, C, D, or E), and pick the one that provides maximum value for the customer and best helps him move at least one step forward in the decision process."

Some sales managers will attempt to discourage independent thinking on your part. You need to actively resist this. Often these sales managers have little direct sales experience of their own. They've read some books about selling and may have attended a couple of training courses, but to them sales is going to be about little more than the process. These people need your help to see that selling is simultaneously a numbers-driven and an interactive, collaborative, and creative process.

Sales is a craft that rewards great creativity. I liken it to storytelling, whether it's writing a novel or developing a screenplay. Each sales opportunity that you work on is a story that needs to be told. And like any effective story, the customer's buying process can be envisioned in three phases: the setup, the conflict, and the resolution.

In the setup phase, your customer's business is humming along. Then there occurs what is called "an inciting incident." In a movie, that might be the scene where a convict, upon release from prison, vows to take revenge on the cop who sent him there. In business, it might be that your customer's accounting system has a hiccup trying to keep pace with the company's growth and experiences a significant failure.

We then move into the conflict phase of the storytelling/buying process, in which your customer is simultaneously using outside consultants to troubleshoot the cause of the system failure, resorting to manual processes to generate invoices, and attempting to define the company's future system requirements in order to initiate the evaluation of new upgraded systems. This is where you, as the seller, get involved in an attempt to understand the buyer's needs.

This brings us to the resolution (or redemption) phase. Based on this particular buyer's situation you have to use your creativity to implement a sales strategy that (1) helps him to better understand his current and future requirements, (2) is completely responsive to his need for information to make a quick decision, and (3) provides sufficient value to motivate him to move with you to the final step of his buying process.

If you are a reactive seller, you'll miss out on the sales opportunities that are stories waiting to be told. The reactive seller often won't recognize the importance of the inciting incident trigger and won't be sufficiently interactive with the buyer to fully understand the requirements and to help formulate an optimal solution. Don't blind yourself to the incredible upside sales potential that can be derived by being an interactive seller.

I had my own experience with the forces of reactive selling that nearly derailed my sales career before it ever got started. Two weeks after starting my first sales job out of college for a major computer company, I was dispatched to a two-week-long introductory sales training class in Pasadena, California. I was going to be trained to sell business computer systems.

My classmates were mostly people who exhibited the sales behavior frequently associated with stereotypical used-car salesmen. They all had firm handshakes, ingratiating insincere smiles, and the ability to bull-rush an objection clean out of the prospect's mind.

At the end of the two-week session, we were sent back to our respective branch offices with a sealed envelope that contained the class instructor's evaluation of our potential for success in sales at the company. A poor evaluation could result in instant termination.

Upon my arrival at the office, I duly handed my envelope to my branch manager and returned to my shared desk in the sales bullpen. A minute later, he stuck his head in the room and motioned for me to come to his office. As I walked in his door, he was leaning back in his chair with his feet up on his desk, reading my evaluation.

"So how do you think training went?"

That sounded like a trick question, but I took the bait. "I thought it went well. I thought I did well."

"Really?"

"Yessir."

"That's interesting you say that because your instructor recommends that we…"—the branch manager paused as he scanned down the page with his finger to find the appropriate sentence—"fire you."

A pregnant pause. I could feel the blood rushing to my face, and a sense of impending doom swept over me. (I remember thinking that I didn't know which would be worse: losing my job or telling my parents I had been fired from my first job after less than a month.)

"Yep, he believes that you will never be successful in sales because you are too . . . analytical. He says you think too much to ever be a good salesman."

The branch manager swiveled in his chair and made a show of dropping my evaluation in my personnel folder in the credenza behind his desk. Then he turned and looked at me. "Well, what are you waiting for? Get outta here and go sell something!" And that is what I have been doing ever since.

CHAPTER 6

Earning Selling Time

IF YOU'RE IN sales, time is your enemy. As much as any other factor, time conspires against you to frustrate and block your success in selling. It is the enemy that hides in plain sight and is largely ignored by most sales managers and salespeople.

Oh, sure, managers and salespeople are painfully aware of time in the context of achieving their assigned daily, weekly, monthly, quarterly, and annual sales goals. Nonetheless, it is a striking paradox that professionals in a field so attuned to time in a calendar sense have so little awareness and appreciation of the critical role it plays in the most basic and fundamental interactions that are intrinsic to consistent sales achievement.

Time doesn't have to be the enemy. It should be one of the most important weapons in your sales arsenal. Time should be the tool you wield to build trust, develop credibility, create value, and truly differentiate you, your company, and your product from those of your competitors. It is a strategic and tactical sales asset. And it will be a vital part of your efforts to elevate your sales capabilities and sales performance to the next level.

Before you can begin to use time to your advantage in your selling, it's essential to understand the role that it plays at the very heart of every sales interaction. The concept may seem a little abstract at first. But once you understand how time works in selling and how customers make decisions about the use of their time, you'll have a simple but powerful tool to use in every sales situation. Ready?

The first thing a customer ever buys from you is time. Before you can even sell your product, the customer must purchase your selling time, which is comprised of your own time as well as the information you can provide to help the customer move closer to making a decision.

The currency the customer will use to purchase your selling time is her time. But strings are attached to the customer's investment. For her investment of time, she has to receive something of value from you in return that is equal to or exceeds her perception of the value of her time. This means that in each instance a customer invests in your selling time, you have to provide value in the form of information that will help move the customer at least one step forward in her buying process.

This simple barter transaction, this exchange of the customer's time for your time and information, is at the heart of every sales interaction. The customer purchases your time. What will she receive in return? What return on investment (ROI) will she receive from you for her investment of time?

If you use the time the customer gives you to provide something of value, what should happen?

"They'll give us more time."

And what will you do with that additional time?

"Continue to sell to them."

Exactly. If you provide something of value in exchange for the time the customer invests with you, then the customer will reward you with additional time to continue to sell to her.

What is a sales call? It is an investment by your customer. And like any investment, there is no guarantee that it will earn a positive return. Your job is to make sure it will. On every sales call, your primary responsibility is to make sure the customer earns a positive return on the time she has invested in you. (In Part III, I'll share tips on how to maximize the value of every sales call.)

Busy people (such as your customers) must make hard choices every day about how to invest their limited time. In 1971, Herbert Simon, an economist at Carnegie-Mellon University—and a future Nobel Prize winner in economics—showed just how they (and we) do this. Simon wrote a prescient description of the upcoming information revolution and the impact that the ready availability of seemingly endless quantities of information would have on our ability to process and use it. Although Simon wasn't specifically addressing the selling and buying of products and services, the conclusions he drew are certainly applicable in today's sales environment:

> [I]n an information-rich world, the wealth of information means a dearth of something else: a scarcity of whatever it is that information consumes. What information consumes is rather obvious: it consumes the attention of its recipients. Hence a wealth of information creates a poverty of attention and a need to allocate that attention efficiently among the overabundance of information sources that might consume it.

Simon was describing a situation based on the laws of economics: The supply of any commodity, in this case the attention span of any consumer of information, is limited, and market forces will efficiently allocate that scarce resource among the various interests competing for it.

Let's apply Simon's lesson to the selling environment. Your prospects and customers are, by definition, consumers of information. They seek it from various sources—such as the Internet, social media, and salespeople—in order to make fully informed decisions about purchasing the right products and services for their needs. However, as Dr. Simon pointed out, customers have a limited supply of attention. At some point during their buying process, they have to make a conscious decision about how to allocate their limited attention bandwidth (that is, their time) among all the demands for that attention, which include vendor relations, administrative tasks, management responsibilities, meetings, phone calls, and e-mails, not to mention texting with their spouses, kids, and friends.

Your prospects make an economic decision about how they are going to prioritize their limited and valuable attention. Sellers who provide the greatest return to the prospect on the time invested in them will have the inside track; they will be given more time to sell. And sellers that waste their prospects' time will not get responses to their e-mails and voice mails—no matter how many e-mails and voice mails they send.

Your customers calculate an economic return on the time they invest in you as a seller. This is called a return on time invested (ROTI). Every sales interaction you have with a prospect is judged on whether it provides value. If you are careless about how you spend the precious minutes your prospects have allocated to you, then they will make the perfectly rational decision to invest their time with another seller. Have you ever wondered why your prospects stopped returning your phone calls or your e-mails? Now you know.

The challenge for you becomes how to effectively cut through the thicket of information your prospects confront and become an asset rather than a liability on their attention's balance sheet. The key is to accelerate your responsiveness. Responsiveness in sales is the combination of content and speed. In Part II of this book, I'll show you how to accelerate your responsiveness by providing the complete and accurate information that your prospects need to move through their buying process in the least amount of time possible. If you do this, they will reward you with the time you need to help them make an informed purchase decision. Help your prospects get their jobs done more quickly, and they will continue to allocate more of their limited time to you because they've learned that you provide better value, and a better ROTI, than your competitors.

CHAPTER 7

Being the Seller Your Customers Need

WHAT'S YOUR sales type? How do you characterize yourself as a salesperson?

How did you answer those questions? Were you compelled to use a traditional, old-fashioned, macho-type sales vocabulary to define your sales type? Are you a "hunter"? Are you a "closer"? Are you "extroverted"? Are you "aggressive"?

Chances are that you describe yourself in these terms because you've convinced yourself that your sales managers want you to embody these characteristics. While your managers might say all the right things about the skills, experience, and personal qualities that typify an ideal salesperson, the informal list of qualifications in the sales manager's mind usually boils down to stereotypical qualities such as:

- Hunter

- Closer

- Extroverted

- Aggressive

Now take a minute and review the definition of selling in Chapter 1. Selling means to provide the information that will help customers make a purchase decision. It means to be the first seller with the answers to the customer's questions, enabling an informed buying decision with the least investment of the buyer's time.

If you think "hunter," "closer," "extroverted," or "aggressive" best describes your sales type, you should ask yourself another important question: Which of those static traits specifically speak to helping customers make purchase decisions? Any of them? Of course not.

- *Hunter:* Are you stalking prey that doesn't even know it's being hunted?

- *Closer:* Are you manipulating or coercing your prospects to sign an order?

- *Extroverted:* Do you possess superficial interpersonal skills that cause customers to be cautious and slow the development of trust?

- *Aggressive:* Are you talking more than listening?

There are real dangers in conforming to old standards of what a salesperson should be. The primary danger is obsolescence. A salesperson is just one of many, many sources of information available to customers to gather data about the products and services they are evaluating for purchase. If you can't provide value by how you sell and help the customer earn a positive ROTI, then you're in danger of losing the customer.

For example, in a 2013 study titled "The Future of IT Sales," researchers from the Gartner Group found that customers, by more than a 2-to-1 margin, would rather deal with a technical specialist or industry expert than a salesperson at each stage of their buying process. Given the choice between technical experts, industry experts, customer support, senior management, and sales, sales was perceived by the customers to provide the least value. This data is both fascinating and disturbing.

If salespeople cannot provide value to a customer, then what role can they play in the customer's buying process? This is why it's critical for you to do an assessment of your sales type and perform an audit of the value that you can provide to your customers.

Based on our compellingly simple and accurate definition of selling, here are four personal characteristics for you to embrace that specifically speak to helping your prospects make better and timelier purchase decisions:

- Responsive

- Curious

- Empathetic

- Problem Solver

It's important to keep in mind that the traditional sales traits such as hunter and closer are like a straightjacket that binds you within a rigid range of responding to prospects. Rather than these static traits that are purely sales focused, it's important to embrace a new set of dynamic sales strengths that are about learning and serving your customer.

"What is your sales type?" is not a trivial question. It's absolutely essential to possess a pragmatic and realistic understanding of your strengths and weaknesses. If you're engaging in self-deception about this, then it becomes extremely difficult to identify and develop the new knowledge, expertise, and skills that will help you take your sales to the next level.

Throughout this book, I'm going to address the four personal characteristics as essential sales strengths, and I'll show how they support the requirements of your prospects.

- *Responsive:* The first seller with the answers wins.

- *Curious:* Success is about the solution the customer needs, not about the product you have to sell.

- *Empathetic:* Understand customers' problems from their perspective.

- *Problem Solver:* Have the knowledge and insights to formulate optimal solutions to the customer's requirements.

How do you get from where you are today to where you want to be? Here are the first two steps:

1. *Become accomplished in at least one area that helps your customer make a decision.* It could be perfecting your product knowledge that you use not only to answer customers' questions but also ask questions of them that will help them better understand their requirements. It could be expanding your industry expertise and your ability to talk about your product or service using industry-specific examples and in a language that resonates with them. Perhaps it's your responsiveness and your ability to marshal the answers and resources that help your customers compress their decision cycle.

2. *Implement your own personal sales improvement plan.* Ask yourself the following question as you embark on improving your selling skills: "Am I the type of salesperson that my customer needs?" In other words, are you the salesperson who can best help your customers achieve their goals? If not, identify those areas of weakness in your skills or knowledge that you need to more fully develop. Seek out the resources that can help you increase your sales performance. It could be taking online courses in a specific field, attending classes to achieve a selling skill or a certification, reading recommended books about selling, finding a mentor, hiring an independent sales coach, or joining a professional association that gives you opportunities to talk with peers and learn how others are selling their products. Seek out the resources your employer has to offer to you, but don't rely on them alone. You've got to be willing to invest time and money in your own success as well.

There's an obvious danger in generalizing about sales types. But you have the responsibility to your company and to your career to make sure that you become a salesperson, not a stereotype. Make it your priority to develop the skills and experience that best support your customers' requirements to make an informed purchase decision in the shortest time possible. And in the process become the type of salesperson with the performance and productivity that both you and your employer need.

CHAPTER 8

Simplifying Your Selling

WE COMPETE IN a complex world where our customers are buried under an avalanche of messages from an ever increasing number of sources, including salespeople like us who are trying to capture just a sliver of their time and attention.

Not only has it become exceedingly difficult for any company to establish and maintain meaningful product differentiation, it has become harder as well to establish meaningful sales differentiation. In the eyes of our prospects, all salespeople look increasingly alike.

As discussed in Chapter 1, this means that the first line of competitive differentiation for any company is not what product or service they sell, but how they sell their product or service. It's how you sell that builds trust, develops credibility around your solution, and provides value to prospects by making it easier for them to make a purchase decision.

Provided, of course, that you actually do make it easier for the prospect to make a decision. Too often I work with salespeople whose sales performance is hamstrung by the very complex sales systems and sales methodologies they employ. The system takes precedence over helping the customer make a decision.

Simplifying your selling provides value to your prospects by making it easy for them to gather the information they need to make their decisions. And it provides value to you, the seller, as well.

In 2013, Siegel + Gale, a New York–based branding firm, released its annual "Global Brand Simplicity Index." Based on its research, the firm found that making it simpler for customers to reach a buying decision paid dividends in three ways:

1. It increased the likelihood of repeat business. (I'll show you why this happens in Chapter 16.)

2. A significant fraction of customers (up to 29 percent depending on the industry) were willing to pay more for "simpler experiences and interactions."

3. Seventy-five percent of customers were more likely to recommend a company that provided simpler interactions.

Siegel + Gale's report concluded that simplicity "brings clarity instead of confusion, decision instead of doubt, and the rewards are real. . . . Simplicity inspires deeper trust and greater loyalty in customers. . . ."

Sales problems can be hard to diagnose, let alone solve. There are many interlocking pieces, and the temptation is to assume that hard problems require complex and expensive solutions. Depending on your company's size and resources, this could mean that your most pressing sales problem doesn't get addressed because there is no budget or that a large investment needs to be made to implement a new selling process and train your entire sales force how to sell to that model.

My experience has shown that a company with sales issues will typically default to the complex solution because managers make the often faulty assumption that the simple solutions are already in place. A company will tend to overlook the simple solutions to their sales problems because they've been conditioned to believe that the only answer to a hard problem costs money. Sometimes this is true, and it requires a reputable sales training and consulting firm to define and implement the fix.

However, more often than not, if management were to do a little digging, they would find that the fundamental disciplines every company needs to execute its sales plan, including those that were believed to have been in place, have either faded due to management inattention or never existed to begin with. They assumed that there was a prompt follow-up to all sales leads. They assumed that all salespeople were immediately and completely responsive to their prospects and customers with answers to questions needed to move forward in the buying process. They assumed that customers were receiving the level of unconditional support required to turn them into loyal repeat customers. They assumed that their frontline salespeople knew their products inside and out, or at least better than their customers did. Well, we all know what happens when you assume.

At this point, you might ask, what this discussion of sales management shortcomings has to do with you.

The answer is that it isn't up to management to make sure that you're executing the sales basics. You shouldn't require a sales manager to force you to follow up sales leads. You shouldn't require a sales manager to prod you to be completely responsive to customer questions or inquiries. You shouldn't require a sales manager to test whether you're keeping abreast of the latest product releases.

The fact is that these simple sales actions are at the heart of selling itself. It is like breathing in and breathing out. You can't do one without doing the other. Just like the autonomic nervous system that controls the involuntary reflex of your breathing, every salesperson needs an autonomic sales reflex that kicks in during core sales situations. Receive a sales lead, follow up now. Get a question, answer it now. One hundred percent of the time.

If you need to, take a minute and review Chapter 1, "What Is Selling?" Remember that your success today is based more on how you sell than what you sell. And the foundation for every salesperson's how is built on the simple things like follow-up, responsiveness, trust, and value. No one but you can control those aspects of your selling. The biggest return on the time you invest in improving your sales performance will come from ensuring that you are mastering these fundamental sales disciplines and incorporating them into your daily routines. Do the simple things first, and the rest will come easily.

Here are three steps that you can take to simplify your selling:

1. *Make every touch count.* Make absolutely certain that each interaction you have with prospects provides value that will help them move one step closer to making a decision. If it doesn't, don't do it.

2. *Be absolutely responsive.* Every customer inquiry or request requires a complete response in the shortest time possible. Don't let a rigid sales process put you at a competitive disadvantage to a responsive seller. Second place in a competitive sales race is no place to be.

3. *Clarify your offer.* Customers have to be able to quickly understand what they can buy from you that will satisfy their requirements. As Einstein was reported to have said, "If you can't explain it to a six-year-old, you don't understand it yourself." If the customer has to work too hard to understand what you are selling, you won't.

CHAPTER 9

Winning the Sale

THIS IS THE FINAL ingredient for your recipe for sales success. There's nothing more important in selling than maintaining an unshakeable focus on . . . well, you know this by now, don't you?

Quick, answer this question: What should be the primary focal point of every step of your sales process? The customer, of course.

But that's only a partial answer. Remember our definition of selling? It's about questions and answers. The customer asks questions in order to gather information to make a buying decision.

As a salesperson, providing that information should inform everything you do. When you plan your sales calls, you know what you need to do. When your manager reviews your accounts and asks you what the next step will be with a particular prospect, you'll have the answer. And if ever you find yourself at a loss for what next step to take with a prospect, you can just ask yourself the question, "What information does the customer need from me right now in order to take at least one step forward in the decision-making process (or buying cycle)?"

There's a lot to be said for taking a long-term perspective in sales. Deals can often take a long time to come to fruition. During parts of my career, I sold multimillion-dollar communications systems with a multiyear sales cycle. But irrespective of the length of the sales cycle/buying process, if you're too focused on winning the order, you may end up losing the sale. I know that may sound confusing. I'll explain.

Let's start with an important factor that you don't learn in sales training: Your customers make up their minds about which seller they're going to buy from fairly early in their buying process. This happens long before they place an order. From that point forward, they are using their buying process to validate that decision. This is not to say that customers have made an irrevocable decision to purchase from particular suppliers. But they've developed a strong preference based on their perceptions of the value those sellers have provided from the beginning of their buying process. (In Chapter 13, I'll show you how to positively influence the customer's initial perceptions of you.)

Such a seller has achieved what I call "winning the sale." She hasn't won the order. That could still take some time. But if she can shepherd the prospect through the rest of his buying process without tripping over herself or making some obvious error, then, to use the old sales cliché, the business is hers to lose. All the other competitors in the deal are wasting precious selling time fighting for second place—and they don't even know it.

If you have worked in sales for any period of time, you've experienced that moment when the customer flips the mental switch and decides that you are the seller he wants to do business with. Personally I know the exact moment that happens in every sales opportunity I work on. I can look back on countless sales calls over the course of my career during which I knew the customer had made the mental decision to work with me. I knew I had won the sale. It still took some time to get the order, though. In one case, it took ten months after winning the sale to finally get the customer's order in hand. But during that time I knew that, if I just continued to maintain my primary sales focus on supporting the customer's decision making, I would indeed win the order.

Unfortunately, short of the prospect's telling you, there's no way to know with 100 percent certainty whether you've won the sale. Over time, your experiences and expertise will blend to give you a reliable intuitive indicator of where you stand. But even then, the only way to sell is as though all your prospects are going to make up their minds about you on your very first sales call.

Which brings us back to your sales focus. I want you to narrow it down just a bit further. If you're going to sell as if your customers were going to make a decision on the very first sales call, then your sales focus needs to be even tighter. Instead of providing information to help customers make a purchase decision, your focus should be on providing value that will win the sale on this call. This value could be in the form of asking the right questions that demonstrate you have a true understanding of the customers' pain points and requirements. The value could come from questions you pose or insights you provide about their business that cause them to reshape their vision of the solution that's required. Or the value could flow from providing thorough answers to their highest-priority questions and concerns.

I want you to remember that winning the sale means that you've helped your customers make a decision. Even if it's a preliminary decision, it's one that they could not have made if you hadn't provided something of value to them. That value could have come from something as mundane as quickly responding to an inquiry or as simple as asking the right questions that demonstrate to your customers that you really understand their requirements. In upcoming chapters, I'll show you how to maximize the value of every customer interaction in order to win the sale on the first call.

It can take a long time to get an order. But with the right focus, it won't take long at all to win the sale.

PART II
Accelerating Your Responsiveness

CHAPTER 10

The Speed of Responsiveness

IN PART I, I TOOK you through all the key ingredients for increasing your sales effectiveness—except for one. I left out responsiveness, which is the single most important skill you must master and integrate into your selling. It's so important that it requires its own section of this book. If you're not completely responsive to your prospects and customers, you'll never reach the sales goals you have set for yourself.

A lack of responsiveness in sales affects companies of all sizes. As you'll learn in Chapter 12, even a company like IBM, a global behemoth with virtually unlimited resources, suffers from poor responsiveness. It doesn't have to be this way. Responsiveness is not only the most important sales attribute to master, but it's also one of the easiest. And, for you, what could be better than having such a simple and practical method for building trust, credibility, and differentiation with your prospects?

Responsiveness has a specific definition in sales. It's the combination of two inseparable elements: information and speed. Take away one element, and you're no longer responsive.

Being responsive to your prospect is about more than just being quick to respond. For instance, if you're fast to respond to your prospect's inquiry but can't provide any data or information that the prospect can use to move forward in the buying process, then you're not being responsive. Being fast is good for gold medals, but in the absence of information, speed is not a virtue in sales.

The easiest way to remember the formulation for complete responsiveness is to see it as an equation:

$$\text{Responsiveness} = \text{Information} + \text{Speed}$$

Speed, obviously, is the time it takes to provide the requested information to a customer. To become a truly responsive seller, speed needs to be measured in minutes or hours, not in days or weeks. We've established that time is in short supply for your prospects. Your performance has to meet or exceed their expectations. It's all too common for salespeople to feel good about themselves when they receive a question from a customer in an e-mail and provide a response the next business day. But what if your primary competitor satisfactorily answers that same question within 30 minutes? What has happened to your competitive position? Has it (a) worsened, (b) improved, or (c) stayed the same? The only realistic answer is a, worsened.

So flip that last question on its head. What will happen to your sales results when you commit to being absolutely and completely responsive to every customer enquiry and request? What will happen to your competitive posture on every deal you work on when your competitors have to struggle to keep pace with your responsiveness? And what will happen to the size of your commission checks when you set your standard to be responsive to all customer questions within an hour as opposed to a business day or a week?

Before we move on to the next chapter, I want you to consider responsiveness in another important light. You probably don't consider the impact of physics on your sales efforts. But you should.

Think of your prospects' buying processes in terms of Heisenberg's principle of uncertainty. Werner Heisenberg, the German physicist and winner of the Nobel Prize in Physics in 1932, is well known, among other things, for his Uncertainty Principle, in which he demonstrated that the act of observing or measuring a process changes its outcome. Although Heisenberg arrived at his famous formulation through his work with the behavior of subatomic particles, I've found that a variation of the Uncertainty Principle applies to sales as well.

According to the Andy Paul Uncertainty Principle of Selling, the process of selling to your prospect invariably changes the prospect's requirements and decision criteria moving forward. The very process of discovery, of helping a prospect define her requirements, and of providing the data and information in response to her questions, forces her to reassess her needs and redefine the criteria she will use in evaluating sellers and making an informed purchase decision.

What happens when you sell to a prospect? What happens as your prospect moves through the decision-making process? What happens when the prospect learns that your product provides a feature and an associated value that she hadn't anticipated when she first put her requirements together? Or what happens when your prospect's expectations for the new machine tool she's looking to acquire aren't fully met by any of the products she has evaluated? The trajectory of the buying process will change, and the information required to make a decision will also change. This necessarily forces immediate strategy adjustments on the part of the seller.

Picture yourself making a purchase decision. Let's say you are buying a home. You began with certain requirements in mind. But as you move through the process of gathering information about various homes, you develop a fuller picture of the various neighborhoods and house sizes that are available in your price range. As a result, your requirements change, and the criteria you established at the beginning of your housing search also change. Suddenly you're armed with a new set of questions that you need your real estate agent to answer.

Why is this uncertainty important to you? Because it reinforces the necessity of being completely and rapidly responsive to your prospects in their search for the information they need to gather and evaluate in order to make good decisions. Too many salespeople fall into the trap of thinking about their sales process and their prospects' buying process as the instructions on a shampoo bottle: just lather, rinse, and repeat. However, your prospect's buying process is anything but a linear, inflexible sequence of static events. It's a living, breathing, dynamic series of questions to which answers typically generate more questions. This places a very real premium on responsiveness.

Embracing responsiveness enables you to quickly and effectively react to changes in the customer's decision-making criteria. This is a quality that every salesperson needs to cultivate and master. It's an essential tool to build trust with prospects, to develop credibility around the solution you're selling, and, most important, to differentiate you in tangible ways from your competitors. All of which lead to more sales.

CHAPTER 11

The New Sales Funnel

WE'RE ALL FAMILIAR with the sales funnel. It's a commonly used metaphor for moving prospects through the stages of your sales process. The funnel was once a useful tool to manage prospective customers, but customers and their buying behaviors have been so significantly transformed over the past 15–20 years that the old sales funnel has become obsolete.

In its place is a New Sales Funnel that more accurately reflects how customers are moving through the stages of their buying processes. But, even more crucially, the New Sales Funnel reflects changes in how your customers need you to sell to them. And at the center of this change are the concept and practice of responsiveness.

In his bestselling book, *Talent Is Overrated*, Geoffrey Colvin shined the spotlight on the major challenge for decision makers. He said, "Getting information pushes at the two constraints everyone faces: it takes time and costs money. Making sound decisions fast and at a low cost is a competitive advantage everywhere."

In other words, *how* customers make a decision becomes a competitive business advantage for them. In Chapter 2, you learned that *how* you sell creates tangible differentiation that provides a true competitive sales advantage for you, the seller. Taken together, this means you can solidify your competitive sales advantage by selling in a manner that makes it faster and easier for the customer to make a decision.

Your customers need you to become a responsive seller by providing them the information they need to make an informed decision in the least time possible. If you can tightly align your selling process with their information needs, you'll be able gain the competitive advantage described by Colvin.

What are your customers' costs of getting information? Primarily, it's the time and cost of the people involved in the process. Think back to Chapter 6. What is the one item that will always be in short supply for your prospects? Time. Customers are always short on time and have to be careful about investing it wisely. For your customers to earn a good ROTI, you have to practice absolute responsiveness. Every minute customers spend on gathering information in their buying process is a minute they can't spend on other profit-making activities. If you make it time-consuming or difficult for customers to get the information they need, you're impeding their ability to compete in their own markets.

Responsiveness is becoming increasingly important to your ability to win business from your customers. For example, let's say there are two sellers, AmpCo and SLO Inc., competing for a big order from DLP Industries. AmpCo's disciplined, rapid sales process provides the information DLP Industries needs at each step of its buying process to make a well-informed and fast purchasing decision. SLO Inc. isn't as organized in its selling processes, with customer requests for information sometimes going unanswered for more than a day or two. Who's more likely to win the business? This focus on responsiveness leads us back to the sales funnel—or what I call the New Sales Funnel.

We all recognize the classic shape of a funnel. In real life, or at least in life outside of sales, funnels are used to transfer liquids from one container to another without spilling. In selling, funnels are meant to transfer potential customers from one stage of the selling process (an interested buyer) to another (a paying customer) without losing them.

The old sales funnel had four distinguishing features, as shown in Figure 11–1. First, there is the broad wide opening at the top to accept all the prospects and suspects that marketing or sales want to throw in there. The second feature is the stages of the selling process that winnow down the number of active prospects. Each of the designated stages is meant to

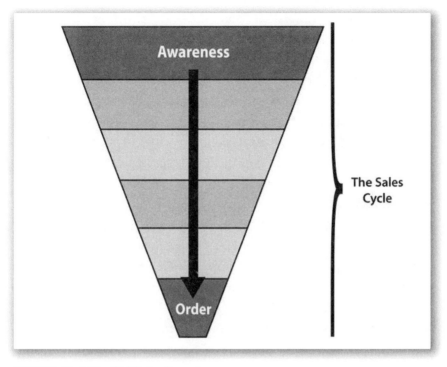

FIGURE 11-1. **The Old Sales Funnel**

represent a milestone on the path to getting an order. As we continue our way down the funnel, we come to the third feature, the narrow neck and small opening at the bottom, representing the exit path for the fraction of prospects that become customers.

The fourth distinguishing feature of the funnel is the most important to you, and that's the way the water backs up to the brim as you pour it in and you wait for it to drain out the bottom of the funnel. That's what happens to most prospects today when they enter the funnel. They wait for a salesperson to respond. Back in the pre-Internet days, waiting was about the only option customers had. If they wanted information about the product or service you were selling, they had to come to you because you were pretty much the sole source of information about those products. But that has all changed.

Today, everyone is familiar with how prospects are largely pre-educated about products and services before they engage with a salesperson for the first time. Studies estimate that in the B2B space, the typical prospects are anywhere from 50 to 75 percent of the way through their buying process before they engage with a seller. They pore over the content on the seller's website, ask questions within their social networks, find user comments and reviews online, participate in LinkedIn discussion groups, and talk with peers on industry forums. This is what I call the Shopping Phase of the buying process. They are searching for and making use of all publicly available information to move as far as possible through the buying process without involving a salesperson.

But there comes a time when customers will have consumed all the publicly available information about a product or service. They will then need a salesperson to help gather the remaining information required to make a sound decision, as well as to help understand the additional questions they should be asking to ensure that they are making a completely educated decision. At that point in time, the Shopping Phase is over, and customers enter the Buying Phase of the decision-making process.

Here's where the New Sales Funnel enters the picture. Some prospects will still enter at the top of the funnel, but increasingly they will enter the funnel at least halfway down (at Point A), as shown in Figure 11–2.

By definition, when customers enter the funnel today, they have less information that needs to be gathered and fewer questions that need to be answered to make a decision—and their timing is urgent. Why urgent? Because they've already invested significant amounts of their own time educating themselves about your product or service. Just because prospects weren't engaged with you, it doesn't mean they weren't actively working their way through the buying process. They can see the light at the end of the tunnel (or is that funnel?).

Here's the problem (and you need to think about what happens now from the perspective of the customer). Having finished the Shopping Phase, the customer reaches out to one or more sellers and waits to receive a phone call back from a salesperson. When that call comes, more often than not that salesperson's default initial interaction with a new prospect is to revert to top-of-the-funnel selling: "Let me tell you about our company." "Let me tell you how we were founded in a garage." "Let me tell you about our products."

You see the problem here, right? Educated prospects, having progressed well into their buying process, are forced to deal with a salesperson who is

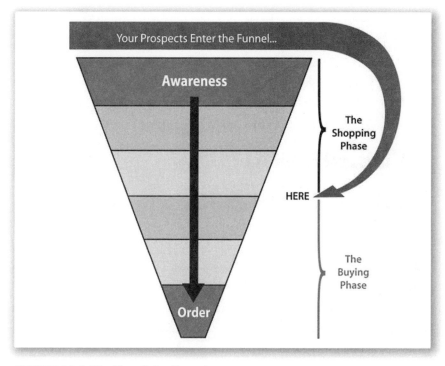

FIGURE 11-2. The New Sales Funnel

unprepared to provide the information they need. Customers have the imperative to make good decisions quickly, and top-of-the-funnel selling just wastes their time. They already have all of that information. They're past that point and are in a hurry to gather more substantive information. Instead of being responsive to customers, you're eroding the possibility of any competitive advantage they might gain from being able to make a fast decision. You're also decreasing your odds of being able to create tangible competitive differentiation that will help you win the order.

So when the customer enters the funnel at least halfway down, there has to be urgency to your selling. You need to hit the ground running, moving at least as fast as the customer. The key to selling to a customer at this stage is responsiveness.

The bottom line for you? What customers need from you has changed. As a result, you need to change how you sell, personally and as a team. The question you need to ask yourself is, "How do I respond to my customers' need for information to make informed decisions quickly?"

CHAPTER 12

Accelerating Your Responsiveness

THERE'S AN EPIDEMIC of poor responsiveness in sales and service. I've known this for a long time as an advisor and consultant to CEOs regarding the sales challenges confronting their companies. What's taken me by surprise in recent years was the depth of the problem.

The most frequent reaction I've heard over the past few years from readers of my first book, *Zero-Time Selling*, as well as from salespeople who have attended my sales training workshops, was their recognition that their responsiveness was woefully deficient. Most surprising of all were the number of similar comments I've received from seasoned, successful, top-grade sales professionals and sales VPs. In many cases, these were people I knew personally, senior sales pros with 30-year track records of sales success in multiple industries, who recognized that they weren't being completely responsive to their customers.

This epidemic doesn't afflict just salespeople. An article in the April 25, 2013, issue of the *Wall Street Journal* reported on an internal IBM video that had been sent to all 430,000 of its employees by CEO Virginia Rometty. In her five-minute missive, Rometty decried the absence of a sense of urgency among her legions in responding to customers. She charged that IBM had not been sufficiently proactive in engaging with its customers to get them answers to their questions. As revealed in the *WSJ* article, the solution was to change IBM's process in hopes of changing its culture: "The CEO then unleashed a new rule. If a client has a request or question, IBM must respond within 24 hours."

By their CEO's reckoning, IBM was a company that had a responsiveness problem. Even a cohort of some of the best trained and best managed sales and support people in the tech industry, with virtually unlimited resources at their command, who design, sell, manufacture, integrate, and deploy some of the most complex IT systems in the world, was visibly failing at this most basic of skills. Consequently, they were becoming vulnerable to their competitors.

Unfortunately, customers have become conditioned not to expect responsiveness. Many reasons contribute to this. Salespeople and their managers might not recognize how essential responsiveness is to their efforts to build trust and credibility with prospects. Most important, they fail to understand how responsiveness at every stage of the customer's buying process creates the foundation for true seller differentiation, which leads to a tangible and sustainable competitive advantage.

The mistake sellers make is in assuming that customers don't place a value on responsiveness. They do. Watch and listen to Virginia Rometty's message to IBM's 430,000 employees. She did not decide out of a misplaced sense of altruism to fix a problem that didn't exist. To the contrary, she was responding to concerns expressed by IBM's customers that the global behemoth couldn't keep up.

It's not just big companies that struggle with poor responsiveness and squander opportunities to win business. Not that long ago, I was shopping online for a particular software service for my company. I spent a few hours researching the alternatives and narrowed my choices to one company's system that seemed to fit my needs. That company was a mature start-up with a recognizable name.

I had a few questions that required answers before I could make a final purchase decision. I tried to find a phone number for their sales department on the company's website but they didn't offer one. So I tracked down an e-mail address for their sales department and submitted a list of five questions. Within an hour I received an e-mail response. At that point I was encouraged. I prefer doing business with like-minded companies. Then I read their response:

> Dear Andy,
>
> Thank you for your interest in XXXXXXXX. We are here to help you. Please let me know if you have any questions.
>
> Regards,
> Dan

Sigh. I bought from another company.

Unfortunately, Dan, like too many other salespeople, doesn't think about responsiveness from the perspective of his prospects and customers.

Chances are good that you compete in a market where it's extremely expensive to create and maintain any meaningful product differentiation. Innovative products and services are quickly copied and commoditized in a rush to market by a myriad of competitors. As a result, in the eyes of your customers, the product(s) that you sell, as well as those your competitors sell, are perceived to be largely the same. In this environment, then, how do you stand out? How can you reliably distinguish yourself from everybody else?

Responsiveness becomes one of the primary tools you can use to demonstrate to your customer that the experience of working with you and your company is different from the others and, in the process, develop a level of credibility and trust that will result in winning orders. If you value responsiveness, then it will quickly become apparent to your prospect through your actions.

What is the measure of responsiveness? How do you know whether you're being responsive? Unfortunately, there's no one answer to this question. The bottom line is that you're being responsive if your customer believes you are. The danger in this approach is thinking of responsiveness as a fixed target. A business environment is constantly evolving, and the standard of what constitutes adequate responsiveness in the eyes of your prospects and customers is changing even as you read this.

In his famous Supreme Court opinion on obscenity in 1964, Justice Potter Stewart wrote, "I shall not today attempt further to define the kinds of material I understand to be embraced within that shorthand description; and perhaps I could never succeed in intelligibly doing so. But I know it when I see it." Your prospects and customers feel the same way about responsiveness. They can't give you a precise definition, but they know it when they see it!

That's not to say you should leave your customers' perceptions of your responsiveness to chance. You have to take deliberate steps to define your own standard and process of responsiveness and create metrics that enable you to measure your performance and improve your process.

Here are four steps you can take immediately to increase your responsiveness to prospects and customers:

1. *Commit to responsiveness as a personal sales priority.* There are no good reasons not to prioritize responsiveness. Just bad excuses. It doesn't require prep work. Just do it. Take the vow today: "My time frame for responding to every customer inquiry, question, or request for help will be immediate." Responsiveness requires a personal effort. Don't fool yourself into believing that an auto-generated e-mail to a customer request is responsive. It isn't; it only contains one of the two required elements of responsiveness. The key to creating sustainable sales-based differentiation is to incorporate complete responsiveness into every step of your selling process.

2. *Set personal and company standards.* IBM took the right first step by creating a standard measure for responsiveness. I give them credit for putting a stake in the ground. While I believe 24 hours is too long to respond to a customer question, establishing an initial metric against which to measure your responsiveness is a great start. Be sure to share your standards with customers and management. You need that additional accountability that comes from publicly committing to a specific standard of performance.

3. *Measure your responsiveness.* I apologize for dragging out the old truism that you can't improve what you don't measure. But it's absolutely true. If you're going to create a metric-based expectation for responsiveness, then you must collect the data to measure. For your personal responsiveness, you can use your CRM system to track this. Or keep a manual diary for a few days to analyze exactly how sharp your responsiveness reflexes are.

4. *Refine your process.* Every day that goes by, the pressure will be on you to become more responsive. Remember the Andy Paul Uncertainty Principle of Selling from Chapter 10? The customer's buying process is a living, breathing, changing thing. Much like the changing competitive landscape that will force IBM to keep reducing the amount of time it requires to respond to a customer, you too must continually improve your responsiveness to meet your customers' requirements. In addition, if you blow away customers with your responsiveness, they will begin to expect it each and every time they interact with you. This third-party accountability is great motivation to keep improving.

Think about it this way: Every hour of the customer's time that you can save in their buying process accrues to their benefit—and to yours. You will have given them time to invest in other profit-generating activities. Therefore, make certain that you blow customers away with your responsiveness. I'm stunned every time I respond rapidly to a customer inquiry, and the customer is shocked that I called them back at all, let alone so quickly. I try to respond to every lead or question I receive within 30 minutes of receiving it. (Here's a helpful tip: When I follow up with a customer, I always begin by apologizing for taking so long to respond. It makes the point. And raises the bar for all your competitors.)

CHAPTER 13

The Power of the First Perception

IF YOU WANT to energize your sales efforts and increase your ability to move a customer to a decision more quickly, you need to focus on making a powerful first impression. And responsiveness, more than any other tool at your disposal, is the most effective method for making that impression.

Your ability to win any order hinges in large measure on the customer's initial perception of the value you're able to provide. And this perception is formed within the first few seconds of your initial interaction. The very first actions you take to shape the buyer's perception of you—their primary point of contact for learning about the products and services you sell—will often spell the difference between winning and losing.

Often, the words "impression" and "perception" are used interchangeably. However, for your purposes, they have distinct meanings that you should understand and integrate into your sales planning.

An impression is something that you give the customer. If you have a new lead that requires follow-up, you're going to plan to take actions that you believe will make a positive first impression. But you don't want to leave this to chance. You have to define in advance specifically what you want that impression to be.

A perception is what a customer senses about your actions. It's an instantaneous and intuitive recognition of the value, or lack thereof, that the customer feels you bring to the buying process. We've all heard the phrase, popularized in the 1980s by the late Lee Atwater, the campaign manager for President George H. W. Bush: "Perception is reality." It's true in sales, where the customer's perception of you is based on the first few moments of your initial interaction. This perception will influence whether you have a fighting chance to win the customer's business.

This first perception in sales is a very close relative to love at first sight. Don't laugh. It's similar to what happens when prospective romantic partners first meet. In a study released in 2010, a team of researchers from the United States and Europe, investigating the neurophysiology of love, used data from brain scans performed on volunteers to develop new insights about what happens during the first few moments of an initial encounter, when impressions are made and perceptions about another individual are formed. In an article published by Syracuse University, the lead researcher, Stephanie Ortigue, PhD, described the speed at which the brain filters sensory input to decide whether someone is desirable:

> It's as if you have an unconscious checklist in your mind: Does this [person] fit my checklist or not? If there is one point that doesn't match, the [person] is rejected. But if he or she passes the first point, then you check the next one and the next one. The thing that's fantastic about the desiring mind is that it all happens so quickly. Within 200 milliseconds our brain knows whether we desire someone—before we know it consciously!

This idea that our brain can make a decision in less than a fifth of a second, before we are consciously aware of it, is called "unconscious perception." This is the intuitive part of the equation. The gut feeling. The customer senses something about you, and makes a decision about your desirability as a supplier of a product or service, before he or she is even consciously aware of it. It's a downright sobering thought. Two hundred milliseconds is about half the time it takes to blink your eyes. Try it. Blink now. Yeah, that's how long it takes the customer to form a perception, positively or negatively, of you and the value you offer.

What do you want his first perception of you, your product or service, and your company to be? Do you want it to be as Shakespeare's contemporary, Christopher Marlowe, asked: "Who ever loved, that loved not at first sight?" Or perhaps it will be as described by Herman Melville: "Contempt is as frequently produced at first sight as love." Personally, I vote for Marlowe.

By now you're probably wondering, "Okay, what is this first perception I need to create?" The Power of the First Perception means that a seller causes the customer to extrapolate from their initial positive experience what the experience of working with that individual would be over the long term (i.e., as a paying customer.) As you'll see, this initial perception is extremely hard to change, so you have to consciously maximize the value and impact of your first impression.

The key is to think about the impression you want to make in terms of what the customer wants. In earlier chapters, you learned how technology and the Internet have changed buying behaviors. You also learned that most customers move a substantial way through their buying process on their own, without the help of a salesperson. But when they reach the point when they have to engage with a seller to move toward a decision, their need and their timing are urgent. So if customers initiate an inquiry, what do they want to happen? They want someone to pick up the phone and call them right now.

Responsiveness is your key to making a good first impression and creating a positive first perception. Customers are acutely aware of responsiveness in sales. They just don't experience it very often. But what happens when you condition customers to expect complete responsiveness from you? As the English poet William Hazlitt said, "We generally make up our minds beforehand to the sort of person we should like . . . and when we meet with a complete example of the qualities we admire, the bargain is soon struck." When your customers perceive that your sales values are in alignment with their own, then you increase your chances of winning their business.

Responsiveness is a distinct competitive advantage in the current commodity-oriented markets. If you value it, your prospects will quickly perceive this, and it will set you apart from your competitors. In Chapter 9, I pointed out the importance of winning the early sale. Using responsiveness to shape the customer's positive first perception of you and your company is a way not only to win the sale but also to do it on the very first sales call.

I once helped a client restructure and refine his sales process to the point where 100 percent of the leads received a follow-up phone call within 30 minutes. Their sales blew up. Their customers just couldn't believe that (1) a seller was responding to their inquiries and (2) they were being called so quickly. As a result, my client's salespeople were winning the sale on a substantial fraction of their initial follow-up calls. Just as important, they learned how little effort was required to use responsiveness to make a compelling first impression.

The same applies to you. Take the actions that are under your control to influence the perception of the customer. Being responsive is the easiest. You don't need approval. You don't need support. You don't need permission. It simply requires some thought about the impression you want to convey and then doing what it takes to make that happen. Like picking up a phone and making a call. Think about this from the customer's perspective:

(1) Responsive presale = Responsive postsale support

(2) Unresponsive presale = Unresponsive postsale support

Two more quick but important points about responsiveness and the Power of the First Perception.

First, perceptions are extremely sticky. That's both good and bad. It's good if your actions create a compellingly positive first perception. On the other hand, if you're nonchalant about the first impression you make, you've got a serious problem.

Research has shown that first perceptions are very difficult to change. According to a 2010 study published in the *Journal of Experimental Psychology*, your first impression of another person, a place, or an idea is automatically locked in as your brain's default perception. Any information that you subsequently receive that runs counter to that perception will not change it. Instead, this contradictory information is treated by your brain as an exception and set aside.

The persistence of a first perception demonstrates the distinct competitive advantage that comes from being extremely prepared to make a good first impression. As long as your actions continue to support the customer's initial perception, your competitors will find that any negative selling on their part will have little impact on the customer's decision making.

This also means that if a customer forms a negative first perception of you, your product, or company, it will be extremely difficult to change. Even if you provide evidence to contradict that perception, it likely will not change. At that point, you will have to consider whether the customer is still worth pursuing.

Second, leading with responsiveness to shape a first perception opens the door to quickly building a trust-based relationship with a customer. Any company that has a website advertising its products or services and publishes contact information or has a Contact Us button is making an implied promise that it will respond to customer inquiries or requests for information. Salespersons who promptly honor that promise and live up to that commitment by responsively following up will win the perception battle and gain the inside track to the customer's business.

PART III
Maximizing Value

CHAPTER 14

Delivering Maximum Value

UNFORTUNATELY, IN the world of sales, the word "value" is in danger of actually losing its value due to overuse. In this part of the book, I'll help you by framing what value means from a customer's perspective—and what it means for you, the seller. In addition, I will give you a simple and practical sales planning tool that will enable you to quickly visualize and maximize the value that you can deliver for your customers at each stage of your selling process.

In the context of selling, value is so loosely defined and randomly tossed around that I suspect it has lost much of its meaning for salespeople. In sales, value has two dimensions, and it is important to understand the difference between them.

Sales literature exhorts salespeople to "provide value" to their customers or to "create value" for their customers, as if the two actions are the same. They aren't. Each is important, and each must be used at various stages in your selling.

Let's start with the definitions of value for sellers. On the one hand, something has value based on its usefulness. On the other hand, it has value based on its quantifiable worth. Worth is a tangible value. Usefulness is less tangible but still quite important in the sales context.

If you *provide* value to a prospect, that value is tied to usefulness. For instance, the value you provide in the form of answers to a specific customer question helps them to move forward in their decision making. Or, conversely, you asked perceptive and effective discovery questions that helped you shape a better solution for the customer (as well as build trust by demonstrating your domain expertise). The value that you provided in these instances was useful irrespective of the speed with which it was delivered.

If you *create* value for customers, the value can be quantified. For example, you created value through your responsiveness at each stage of your selling, which enabled the customer to compress the length of the planned buying cycle by 30 days. Or you created value by showing the customer a different approach to meeting his or her requirements, which could create a critical and sustainable advantage in the customer's core market. The value that you created was tangible and quantifiable.

Irrespective of which type of value you deliver to your customers, you have to bear in mind that value doesn't happen by accident. It is the result of deliberate planning and preparation. If you want to consistently achieve a high level of success in sales, you have to plan every interaction with a customer to provide or create the maximum value with the least possible investment of the customer's time. This is a perfect match with the customer's desire to make informed decisions quickly and at a low cost.

Delivering maximum value through your selling means that the day of the ad hoc sales call is dead. Say good-bye to winging it. Every sales interaction, large and small, has to be planned for maximum value. It doesn't matter whether it is an in-person meeting, phone call, video chat, e-mail, text, or Tweet. Every sales interaction needs a value plan.

This puts the burden on salespeople and sales managers alike to ensure that the planning occurs. It doesn't require a 30-minute meeting to plan an e-mail, but it does require thought and preparation.

Here are two simple questions that you need to answer to guide your planning and preparing for your next customer interaction:

- *What is the goal of this call/contact?* In other words, what is the exact value that you are going to deliver to the customer? This has to be identified up front, and your sales approach has to be prepared to ensure that you effectively execute your plan and achieve the goal of the call.

- *What is the desired outcome of this interaction?* What steps do you want customers to take or what decision do you want them to make? Especially in the case of face-to-face interactions (whether virtual or in person), it is good practice to set an expectation that if you deliver the promised value, customers will take an agreed-upon step forward in their buying process.

Without this planning, you run the risk of committing the cardinal sin of selling: wasting the customer's time. We have already established that your customers don't have a minute to spare. If customers give you their time, what will they receive in return?

The fact is that every interaction you have with a customer is judged to be either a win or a loss. After the call, customers will ask themselves, "Was this a good use of my time or not?" If you end up with too many checkmarks in the loss column, then you will find that the customer no longer has time for you. She'll have decided that she cannot earn a positive return on the time invested in you.

Recently, I was in the market to buy a bicycle. I passed a bike store in Manhattan, not too far from where I live, and was struck by a gorgeous bike displayed in the window. It had a unique and appealing geometry. The store had just opened, and I was the only customer. Two sales clerks sat behind the register about 20 feet away. I looked at the bike in the window display. Two minutes passed, and neither clerk approached me. Hmmm. I decided to test them. I turned and walked the length of the store to the back room where more bikes were available. As I passed the register one of the clerks gave me a slight "What's up?" head nod. That was all. I spent five minutes in the back room, stalling, waiting to see whether someone would come sell to me. Nope. I walked back through the store and out the door, and not a word was spoken. I bought my expensive bike from another store a week later. I would have preferred to buy it from the store I visited because of its convenience but decided I didn't want to risk wasting more time there.

Another example that should be familiar to everyone: the classic check-in call. Assume that it's been a couple weeks since you've been able to communicate with a good prospect. You're beginning to get a bit nervous, so you pick up the phone. "Hey, Mr. Prospect. Hi. Yes, this is James from AB Co. . . . Fine. How are you? . . . Well, thanks for taking the call. No, I don't really have anything new. It's just that it's been a couple weeks since we last talked. . . . I know, time flies. . . . Well, I just wanted to check in . . . ."

Raise your hand if you've ever made a check-in call on a customer. C'mon, let's see a show of hands. If you're in sales, and you don't have your hand up, then you're not being honest with yourself. The fact is that we have all made check-in calls. Our customers gave us their time, and what did we give them in return? Nothing. Nada. Bupkes.

This behavior has to stop.

It is not the objective of your customers to spend time with you. In fact, the opposite is true. They want to accomplish their aims, which is to buy a product or service, while spending as little time with the salesperson as possible.

Salespeople often fall into the trap of believing that doing something—anything—with a prospect is better than doing nothing. For instance, this happens when the prospect has gone radio silent. There are lots of reasons why this could occur, and it is your job to determine why. Oftentimes the customer is waiting on you to supply information to help move to the next stage of the buying process. Find out what the customer needs and respond appropriately with content that has the value at that moment. Rarely is the correct response to bombard the prospect with time-wasting requests and trivial sales interactions.

In fact, nothing is better than something. If you don't have a plan to maximize the value of a customer interaction, just don't do it. If you don't have a specific value plan for a customer phone call, don't make it. If you don't have a value plan for an e-mail you are thinking about sending to a prospect, don't send it. You know the risks involved with wasting your customers' limited time. So what is the downside of not wasting a customer's time? None.

By delivering maximum value, you are enabling sales. But I rarely ever hear salespeople specifically state that, as part of their account plans, they are going to provide value or create value for their customers. It's time for that to change. As I've stressed throughout this book, successful selling is a deliberate act. The top salespeople are mindful of the actual value the customer will receive from each sales interaction. Taking the right steps to maximize that value is an effective strategy to enable and amplify your sales success.

CHAPTER 15

Visualizing Value

THE BEST WAY to learn about maximum value selling is to see what it looks like. Figure 15–1 is a generic sales process. The horizontal x-axis, TIME, measures the duration of the sales process and all the individual sales touches. The vertical y-axis, VALUE, measures the value received by the customer during each step in that process.

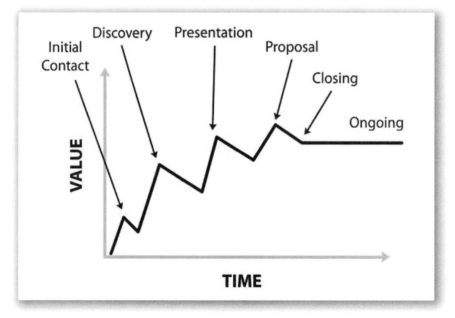

FIGURE 15–1. The Typical Sales Process: Building to the Close

First, note how each little peak in the process signifies a touch, or a customer interaction. It is represented as a peak because the value that you can deliver occurs during a sales interaction. When you are not in front of the customer, either in person or virtually, there will be an inevitable drop in value. After all, what is the first thing customers do once you leave their office? They start forgetting about you—until your next interaction with them.

Which brings us to the next characteristic of the sales process. If you are effectively providing or creating value during your interactions, then there should be a gradual buildup of residual value throughout the length of your sales process. That is why the ending point of your process is higher than the starting point, which occurs prior to your first interaction with the customer.

I am often asked why the last touch, usually receiving an order, is lower in perceived value than the other touches throughout the process. It's because, in most cases, the customer makes the decision without the salesperson being present. It's why the trope of closing an order is one of the biggest fallacies in selling. In the B2B space, very rarely are salespeople in the room when the customer makes the final decision about which product to buy. If the salesperson isn't present, then value can't be delivered. Thus, the closing touch is lower.

Lastly, as you can see, the sales process extends beyond the closing. This is your ongoing postsales account management and customer support. If customers have questions after giving you the order, you need to be as responsive as if you were still working to earn their business. That's because any interactions in this phase of the sales process are actually the first sales calls for your next order from the customer.

Now let's take a look at what a typical competitive process looks like. As I described in Chapter 1, we're all working in an increasingly challenging business environment where the number of competitors in each segment is quickly rising, where it is difficult to establish and maintain any meaningful product differentiation, and where all vendors essentially look alike to the customer. Earlier in this book, when I provided strategies to create tangible differentiation in your selling, it was to overcome this very problem.

Unfortunately, most salespeople are not differentiating their selling either in the value they deliver or in their responsiveness to the customer. Figure 15–2 shows a typical competitive sales process with four vendors. Each goes through roughly the same steps to provide roughly the same information to the prospect. As you can see, the various threads are often bunched on top of one another. If you were the prospect, would you be able to distinguish one seller from the other, or would it all sound like white noise?

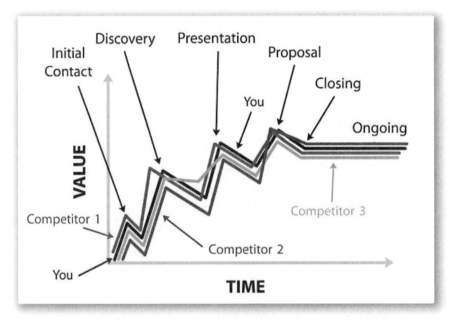

FIGURE 15–2. Most Competitors Look Alike to Buyers: Your Message Gets Lost in the Noise

Most of us are familiar with white noise. I remember watching TV as a kid, before we had cable, when the channels would go off the air at some prescribed time in the middle of the night. If you turned on the TV, all you'd see and hear would be a flickering screen flecked with random bits of black and white and a somewhat harsh staticky noise. That nonspecific sound was white noise.

Figure 15–3 shows a graph of white noise side by side with your competitive sales process. Kind of eerie, how similar they are, isn't it? Insomniacs

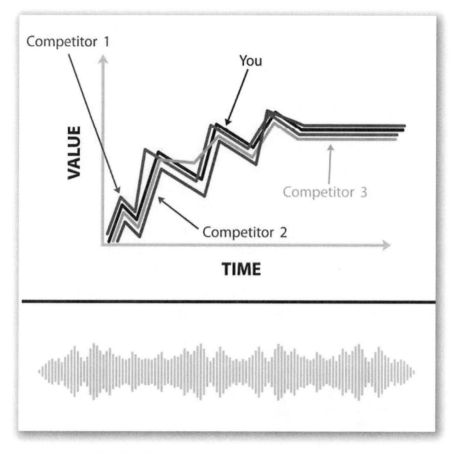

FIGURE 15–3. **Don't Let White Noise Be the Only Thing Your Prospects Hear**

buy white noise machines that generate soothing, nonidentifiable sounds to lull them to sleep. It's ironic that a pack of undifferentiated salespeople can have the same effect on a customer.

When your customers hear white noise, it means that they are not being given the information that will help them choose one vendor over another. This often leads to the customer's making the dreaded no-decision decision: "We didn't get what we needed from any of the vendors. So we're just going to hold off on this decision for a bit." To prevent putting your customers to sleep, you need to step up your game and create some true differentiation throughout your selling process (and the customer's buying process.)

Consider this process from the customer's point of view. As described in previous chapters, customers want to make decisions faster and at a lower cost. A study published in 2013 by IDC surveyed executives in companies in the IT industry and found that they wanted to make buying decisions 40 percent faster! That is a significant fraction of time to lop off their buying process. Some of the time savings will necessarily come from improved internal buying processes. But the bulk of the time they'd like to save has to come from the sell side.

So let's take our standard sales process graph and see what happens when we compress it by 40 percent. In Figure 15–4, you can see the compressed buying process that your customers want. For comparison purposes, I've laid it on top of the standard sales process. The upper track is what customers want and need from salespeople. They need each touch, each interaction with a salesperson, to provide more value, and they need all the value delivered over a shorter period of time.

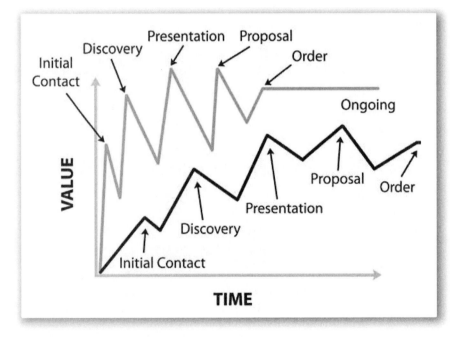

FIGURE 15–4. The Maximum Value Selling Track: Maximize Value, Responsiveness, and Speed

Look at the graph, and measure the distance between the peak for the upper track and the lower track for the first sales touch. That is called the Value Gap (Figure 15–5). The Value Gap is the difference in value received by the customer between Touch 1 on the upper track and Touch 1 on the lower track. Look at this as a competitive sales situation, where you are on the upper track and your most challenging competitors are on the lower track.

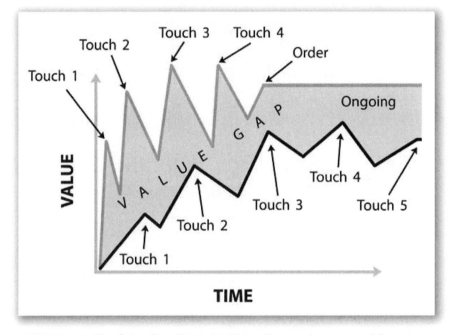

FIGURE 15–5. The Value Gap: Maximize Value, Responsiveness, and Speed

Next, in Figure 15–6, you have risen above the noise created by your competitors and opened this Value Gap starting with the very first interaction. The Value Gap is comprised primarily of the more complete and timely information you have provided that customers need to move forward with making a decision. It includes the unique insights that you have provided that helped to perfect customers' vision of the solution that will meet their requirements. Just as important, it contains the elevated levels of trust, credibility, and confidence that the customer has in you, based on your continued focus on responsiveness and value.

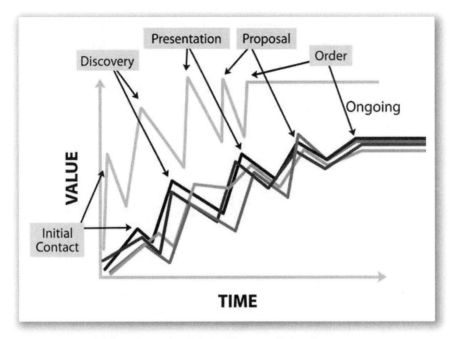

FIGURE 15–6. Rising above the Noise to Create a Value Gap

For instance, let's assume that Touch 1 was responding to a sales lead. The salesperson on the upper track responded within an hour, asked effective discovery questions, and scheduled a follow-on call to demonstrate her system. The salesperson on the lower track took two days to respond to the lead with a phone call (which, unfortunately, is pretty average). He opened the call with the typical top-of-the-funnel look-at-me sales presentation and eventually got around to asking about the customer and his requirements. The customer ended the call without committing to a next call. "Give me a couple of days to digest this. I'll get back to you." What's in the Value Gap? Information, trust, credibility, and confidence that you won't waste the customer's time.

I have three action items for you before we move on to the next chapter.

First, I want you to go back and look at the standard sales process in Figure 15–2. Think back to Chapter 11 and our discussion about the customer's motivations in decision making: faster and at lower cost. What would your process look like if you took the necessary steps to meet the customer's requirements for faster decision making? You would attempt to increase the value of each interaction, and you would attempt to deliver the value that the customer needed to make their decision in less time. What would your selling cycle look like then? It would look just like the upper track in Figure 15–4. This is the Maximum Value Selling track. And it is perfectly aligned with the preferred buying process of your customer. This is not an accident.

Second, develop your own sales process graphs. When you sit down to plan any sales interaction (in-person call, phone call, video chat, e-mail, text, Tweet), map it out on the graph. Ask yourself these questions:

- What is the goal of this sales interaction (as defined by the value you will deliver)?

- Is this the maximum value I can deliver during this call/contact?

- What is the desired outcome(s) of this interaction?

- If I am delivering less than maximum value, what will happen if a competitor delivers the maximum value at the same stage?

Third, graph what your selling process looked like for the last deal you lost. How many touches of all types were there? What was the relative value that each delivered? What was the relative length of time between each one? Then map in the track of the competitor that won the deal. Where were the Value Gaps that you fell into?

CHAPTER 16

The Peak/End Rule of Sales

IT'S TIME TO ADD a little more science to your selling. You've probably noticed that I have referred to various scientific studies and surveys throughout this book. My objective is to help you understand the logic and science behind how buying and selling work. At the same time, I want to challenge you to think differently about how selling and buying fit together and about how you should integrate this new knowledge into your own sales efforts—especially in how you plan and execute your sales strategies with your customers.

Now for something that will really transform how you think about your selling process.

Daniel Kahneman is a Nobel Prize–winning economist who is famous for his work on decision making and behavioral economics. Through his research on how people make decisions, Kahneman developed what he called the Peak/End rule. In *The Paradox of Choice*, Swarthmore College Professor Barry Schwarz presented a succinct description of the Peak/End Rule: "Kahneman showed that what we remember about the quality of our past experiences, both good and bad, was almost entirely determined by how the experiences felt when they were at their peak (best or worst) and how they felt when they ended. We use the peak-end rule to summarize the experience and to remind ourselves how the experience felt."

In a paper from 1999, Kahneman describes one study in which participants in a laboratory were asked to listen through headphones to what he described as "a pair of intensely unpleasant noises." The first noise was 10 seconds long at 78 decibels (approximately the volume of a garbage disposal). The second noise was the same 10 seconds also at 78 decibels, followed by four seconds at 66 decibels (roughly the volume of a vacuum cleaner). When presented the chance to choose which of the two noises to listen to again, the overwhelming majority of the participants chose the longer one. On the surface, that choice would appear to be counterintuitive. But in the first noise, the peak experience and the end experience were the same: a loud, annoying noise. The end experience of listening to the second noise was less unpleasant than the end experience of the first noise, so that's what the participants chose. As Kahneman summarized, "People choose to repeat the sound they dislike least, and the Peak/End rule determines that."

The implications of this are very exciting for salespeople who are serious about amping up their selling. Do you see the value that the Peak/End rule provides? In selling, it means that when your customers arrive at the conclusion of their buying cycles and are summarizing their experiences with the various sellers competing for their business, their feelings about you (your product and your company) will be "almost entirely determined" by the peak experience (good or bad) that you created for them during their buying process and by the most recent experience the customer had with you.

This finding is consistent with everything we know about customers in today's business and consumer environments. They are extremely busy and short on time. They are pressed to make better decisions faster. Meaningful differences between products shrink as more suppliers enter the market in every product category. And every seller looks the same.

When the time arrives to make a decision, customers will consider all the tangible factors that might distinguish your offering from those of your competitors. But mostly, they will recall the peak experience from the selling process and their most recent interaction with you. And they'll use that as a basis for her deciding whether they want to buy from you. After all, if the peak experience of working with you during the buying process was negative, then customers will likely not choose to repeat it.

Remember how in Chapter 1 I told you that your success in sales will be determined more by how you sell than what you sell? The Peak/End rule proves it. You have the imperative to take deliberate sales actions that will create the peak experiences that make your selling memorable to the customer.

Figure 16–1 shows the ordinary sales process again. It's hard to see where the peak experience is for the buyer. In the graph, the seller is just going through the motions, doing what he thinks needs to be done but not thinking about what the customer needs.

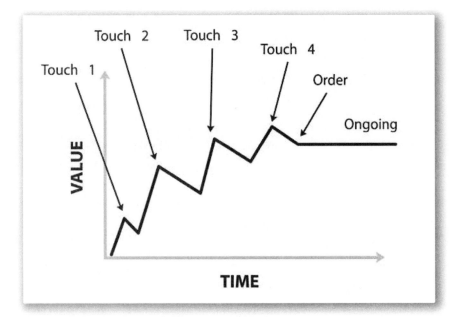

FIGURE 16-1. The Standard Sales Process: Where Are the Peak Experiences?

In this next graph (Figure 16–2), we have the Maximum Value sales process laid over the standard sales process. Suddenly it starts to make some sense, right? Each of the customer touches on the upper Maximum Value track represent potential peak events in the customer's buying process. The Value Gap is created by a maximum value sales touch. In other words, at that stage in the customer's buying process, the incremental value you delivered compared to the competitor's would potentially be a peak event.

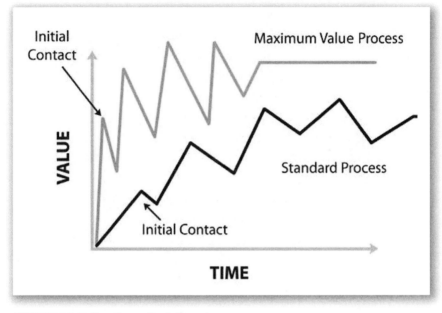

FIGURE 16–2. Creating a Peak Experience

I am often asked two questions about this: "How can you know in advance which touch will be the peak event? And how do you plan for it if you don't know that?" The short answer to both questions is the same: You can't. Every customer touch has the potential to be the peak experience. Therefore, you should plan and execute each and every sales interaction, no matter how big or small, as if it will be the peak experience for the customer.

Take a seemingly innocuous sales action such as a sales lead follow-up. It happens right at the beginning of your sales process. Everyone does it. Or do they? Various studies have found that anywhere from 40 to 70 percent of sales leads are not followed up. So the very act of responsively following up has the potential to be surprising and memorable to your prospective customers.

Look at Figure 16–2 again. On the upper Maximum Value track, the sales rep followed up faster than the rep on the lower Standard track. She quickly researched the company before calling to learn about the business and potential challenges it may face. She also checked through the LinkedIn profile of the requestor to check his or her job title and determine whether they had shared connections. She may have provided value during the call, but she almost certainly created value by being immediately responsive. On the Standard track, the sales rep didn't prioritize the follow-up. He did little prep work, and when he made the follow-up call, he wasn't prepared to focus on the customer and defaulted to talking about his own company, not the customer's.

Michael is an acquaintance who is a VP at a tech company that was undergoing an intense growth spurt and was hiring a lot of people. At one point they were inundated with unsolicited resumes that job seekers were submitting online. The executive management team decided to invest in a cloud-based system to track the resumes and applicants. Tasked with investigating potential solutions, Michael invested a Saturday of his own time to research the available software options. After four hours of research, he had it narrowed down to three companies. Using the Contact Us form on each of the companies' websites, he entered his name and title and wrote a detailed message to explain his requirements, reinforce the urgency of his situation, and request a call by a salesperson ASAP. A full business week passed before he received the first response from any of the three vendors.

That salesperson seemed a little confused when Michael informed him that they were going to stick with their current system for the time being. Hadn't Michael just sent his company an e-mail stating that he urgently needed their solution? Michael agreed that he had. But he said that if it required the better part of a week just to respond to his urgent sales lead, then he couldn't imagine how long it would take them to respond to a customer service request once his company had purchased their system. He didn't need that headache. Instead, he figured out a way to cope with the volume of resumes they were receiving with their existing manual system. Six months later, Michael's company invested in a solution to manage and track applicants. None of the three vendors he had originally contacted were given the chance to bid on his business a second time.

Had a salesperson from any of the three companies that Michael originally contacted followed up with him with the first 24 hours, it would have been a peak experience that Michael would have remembered at decision-making time. As it was, when the first sales rep finally followed up nearly a week after the contact request was submitted, it became a peak event in the negative sense.

Always remember the Peak/End rule of selling, and don't let it work against you.

CHAPTER 17

Delivering Value with Peak/End Selling

WHAT ARE YOU doing to create peak events and make your selling memorable? How can you create a Value Gap with each sales interaction? To answer these questions, let's look back at some of the important sales topics we have covered so far.

Creating a positive first perception. It doesn't matter what form your first contact with the customer takes. It could be a cold call, a meeting at a networking event, responding to a sales lead, or a referral from another customer or mutual acquaintance. Always be prepared to make a first impression that will create a positive perception of you, your product, and your company. I once worked with a salesperson, John, who reliably created a positive perception and a peak event in the minds of his customers by asking during their first interaction what he called his "killer question." This question would expose a gap in the customer's thinking about the requirements, leaving customers to wonder why they hadn't thought of it themselves. It was a great trust-building step that was memorable for the customer when the time came to make a purchase decision.

Immediate responsiveness to inquiries and questions. If customers have been trained through the years not to expect responsiveness from salespeople, just imagine how they feel when they get it. It is a memorable event. As mentioned previously, IBM has set a standard for responsiveness that it feels will differentiate itself from its competitors. Now just imagine if IBM could turn that 24-hour window into one-hour responsiveness. That would be a peak event for customers. I implemented a process for one of my clients that enabled it to respond to every sales lead within 30 minutes. This became a peak experience that often won the sale on the first call.

Discovery. Demonstrate deep domain expertise and business acumen with the quality of the probing questions you ask about the customer's industry, business, and specific requirements. Build your expertise to a level where you can create "aha" moments in the customer's mind by asking questions about the requirements and business objectives that the customer hadn't thought of. Causing customers to change their thinking about what would constitute the best solutions to meet their needs leads to peak experiences.

Shaping the buyer's vision. We will get into this in detail in Chapter 18, but in short, it means shaping the vision in customers' minds of the optimal solution that will meet their needs. This process begins during the discovery stage of your selling process. As you'll learn in the next chapter, this is a peak event with a demonstrable payback for the salesperson who can make it happen.

Provide meaningful insights and context. These days, customers have no shortage of content to analyze about the products and services they are evaluating for purchase. But they may require more information to help them make decisions. Illuminate customers' problems and the decisions that they must make by using third-party information to provide insights and a context for that decision. The Internet is full of information (white papers, industry reports, industry surveys, academic reports, news articles) that can create a context for a decision in relation to overall trends in the customer's industry relating to technology, operations, marketing, sales, distribution, capital investments, and competitors, among others. The value you deliver through context can be decisive for customers in their decision making and therefore a peak experience.

Stories. Well-crafted sales stories are another source of context. The best are concise tellings of how an existing customer is gaining tangible value from using your product or service. These stories can often trigger a deeper understanding of the value of the solution you are selling. Follow the story format that I lay out for you in Chapter 37, and your stories will be valuable and memorable.

Delivering a peak experience is half the battle. Making your last, or end, interaction memorable for the customer is essential as well. Creating the peak event often results in winning the sale, as explained in Chapter 9. But winning the sale or providing a peak experience for the customer is no guarantee that you will win the order. It means that you just need to work that much harder to lock in your advantage by finishing strong and making your last interaction count.

What should be the last interaction you have with customers before they make their decision? And does it really make a difference?

Yes, it does really make a difference. A story often told about the Peak/End rule has to do with taking a vacation. Two people, Jack and Jill, took vacations on Maui with their spouses. Jill stayed for two weeks and went whale watching, took a sunset cruise, and went snorkeling with sea turtles during the first week. Then for the second week she stayed by the pool or beach to catch up on her reading. Jack was on Maui for only a week. He golfed, went whale watching, snorkeled, and on his last day went with a tour to the 10,000-foot summit of Mt. Haleakala to see the sunrise and then rode a bicycle down the mountain all the way to the ocean. Jill's vacation began strong but ended on a quiet note. Jack's vacation had some good moments but ended with an incredible experience cruising down the side of a volcano. Of the two, who had the more pleasurable memory of their vacation? Studies of the Peak/End rule show that it would accurately predict that Jack would have the more pleasurable memory of Maui. As Schwarz says in his book, the Peak/End rule demonstrates that we evaluate our experiences based on "how good they feel at their best, and how good they feel at the end."

I believe that the best way to finish your sales process is to ask what I call "closing questions." I don't mean, closing-the-order questions. Asking a closing question is not the same as asking for the order. In fact, you can pretty much guarantee yourself that asking for the order is neither a peak event nor a positive memorable last sales interaction for a prospect.

Closing questions are the questions you ask to verify that there are no gaps in your understanding of the customer and the problem that needs to be solved, the customer's understanding of your product or service and the value that it will deliver, as well as to ensure their understanding of your proposal and how it will meet his or her business and financial objectives. In addition, closing questions ensure that the customer has used the right assumptions in her internal analysis of your offer. My experience of more than 30 years has shown me that customers are reluctant at the end of your selling process and their buying process to admit that they don't fully understand the details of your proposed solution. Incomplete information can be problematic for your chances of winning.

Closing questions attempt to verify that the customer has enough information to make a decision. Examples include:

- "At our first meeting you stated that you needed a cost-effective method to improve control over critical production processes. Do you understand how our solution will provide the needed process improvements, as well as the IRR (internal rate of return) on your investment, which exceed your stated requirements?"

- "I have this spreadsheet that we have developed to help our customers project the financial returns from their investment in our solution. Have you performed this calculation yet? Let's take a few minutes to enter some of your assumptions and verify that we can meet your internal financial hurdles."

- "Earlier I provided you with a detailed project plan and installation management guide. Do you understand how our solution will integrate and improve the performance of your current systems? . . . With your permission, I'd like to take a few minutes to review some of the key implementation steps with you."

Closing questions are like discovery questions; you have to be professional but direct. Customers rarely volunteer their lack of understanding. You must be sensitive to them and to their perception of the time you are using. But you don't want any competitive advantage that you created through peak experiences to disappear if customers decide they can't buy from you because they have incomplete information.

Your closing questions will leave the customer perceiving you as a detailed, customer-centric professional. By focusing on clearing up lingering questions or uncertainties, you will have created value by making it easier for the customer to reach a decision faster. Think about what the customer's perception of you will be at that moment compared to that of a competitor who is just asking for the order without making sure that the customer has gotten all the necessary information.

One final point about Peak/End selling. During the annual Tour de France bicycle race, there is another competition taking place within the overall competition. At the top of each major climb during the 22-day race, points are awarded to the first rider to reach the summit. The rider who wins the most points on climbs throughout the race wears the distinctive white-and-red polka-dotted jersey to signify his status as the King of the Mountains.

Similarly, in selling you want to be King of the Peaks. The peaks are those moments in the sales process at the apex of a customer interaction. They are the moments you use to create the maximum value for your prospects. These are opportunities to set yourself apart from the competition, to rise above the noise, to help your prospect move closer to making a decision, and to put yourself in the lead position to win the deal.

CHAPTER 18

Shaping the Buying Vision

REMEMBER THAT little sports car that you have always coveted? How many times have you pictured yourself sliding behind the wheel, sitting in a handcrafted leather seat that fits you like a glove, with the dials and gauges arrayed around you as in the cockpit of a fighter jet. You slip the car into gear and—with the top down—head for the nearest open road. You're driving fast down Highway 1 from Carmel to San Luis Obispo, hugging the curves of the California coast, the warm sun on your face and the wind blowing through your hair. Or maybe you want to test the car's nimble handling, so you envision yourself putting it through its paces as you negotiate hairpin turns on the switchbacks over the 9,045-foot Stelvio Pass in Italy.

All that daydreaming has a purpose. You are envisioning what it will be like to own and operate that sports car. By taking it on mental test drives, you are also working through the financial and value justification you'll have to present to your spouse about how this is not just a midlife crisis but a solution that meets your transportation needs ("Sweetie, trust me, I'm sure the kids can squeeze in the back . . .").

This is known as your "buying vision" or "buyer's vision." You've created a detailed story in your mind featuring the various benefits, along with the real and psychic value, you would receive from owning and driving that car.

We all create buying visions. Whether we are buying something practical or indulging our midlife crises, we will mentally picture what it will be like to have that purchase in hand. Thinking about where to eat tonight? In your mind, you're already eating that juicy gourmet burger at the new brewpub in town. Attending a fund-raising gala next week? In your mind, you're already wearing that designer dress you saw marked down 40 percent this morning.

The same holds true for your customers. At some point in their buying processes, they are going to develop a vision of what it will be like to use a product or service like yours. They are going to picture how your product or service operates. They will develop a mental model of the operational benefits and financial payback your product will generate. They will envision the competitive advantages that will be created by using your product. They will have a vision of the impact your product will have on their employees and internal resources. Not least of all, customers will develop a vision of what the successful use of your product or service will mean for them personally.

This buying vision doesn't materialize out of thin air. It's a story of potential and possibilities that is constructed out of the information and insights that you supply to the customer. Like every story, it has a beginning, a middle, and an end. In the beginning, the customer has requirements in the form of a problem or pain point that needs to be addressed. In the middle, the customer uses your product to address the pain points. In the end, the customer is successful and reaps the business and personal benefits from the decision to use your product.

The buying vision is very important to you for four reasons. First, creating the buying vision for the customer is a peak event. In a competitive sales situation, if you rise above the others to successfully move the customer to buy into your vision, then you have created a memorable event. And that memory will be reinforced by what the customer does at the following point.

Second, a buying vision gives your customer a tool to become an effective internal advocate for you. Enthusiastically armed with a buying vision, your customer has something tangible in hand—a story to tell in order to sell internal peers and superiors. Obviously, you want this internal advocate to tell the story with your product in the starring role.

Third, shaping the buying vision improves your chances of winning the business. A research study by the Forrester Group found that the seller who was successful in shaping the customer's buying vision ultimately won the deal an astounding 65 percent of the time!

Fourth, as much as people are reluctant to change their first perceptions of a seller, even when confronted with information that counters that perception (see Chapter 13), trying to change buyers' vision after they have committed to a particular narrative is also very difficult. It can be done, but the odds are against you. This means that you should position yourself to be the seller who shapes the buyer's vision.

What are the keys to creating your customer's buying vision? Let's look at this in the context of potential peak experiences that you can use to influence the customer.

- *Be transparent with your information.* Chances are that customers have already begun to form their vision based on their research before you ever communicate with them. Ninety percent of B2B buyers do some form of online research before they engage with a seller. Before their first meaningful discussion with you, based on the information that they were able to glean from your website and other sources, customers will have begun to develop a preliminary sense of how your product would work for their businesses. Therefore, it is critical that the information you present on your website be as comprehensive and clear as you can make it. In other words, stop hiding information and forcing customers to talk with a salesperson before they are ready.

- *Be first.* Recall all the reasons I've given you for being first: responsiveness, first perceptions, satisficers, building the buying vision. You have a significant advantage being first. How many more reasons do you need? Oh, yeah, if you shape the buying vision, you have a 65 percent chance of winning the order. Keep in mind that buying visions don't have to be comprehensive. But being first is critical! If you hit the major touchstones, then the satisficers—the decision makers who make the good-enough decisions—will have little incentive to keep on looking. They have a story that works for them. They can sell this.

- *Question authority.* Ask pertinent questions that force customers to rethink the assumptions that are the foundations of their buying visions. Customers may be the authorities on their business, but you need to be the expert on your product and how customers use it to optimize the value and the return they receive from it.

- *Provide wisdom.* Use your domain expertise to build a position as a trusted source of important insights. Customers gather a lot of content. They get overwhelmed and ask, "Why is this information important to me, and how does it apply to the specific decision that I have to make?" They need your insights to help them fully understand the relevant context for that content. For example, these can come in the form of market research reports or case studies. Your insights will have more value if you look beyond your own set of customers and experiences and search for what other similar companies have done.

- *Tell great stories.* Well-crafted and well-told sales stories are one of the most effective ways to convey information about why buyers chose your product and how they received value. Sales stories provide an important source of context. A customer in a related industry, with similar business challenges, in the same business climate made the decision to go with your product and your company. Understanding the reasons why that customer chose you provides context for your buyer.

Lastly, what happens if you encounter a prospect that already has formed a buying vision prior to your first engagement? Say the buyer has been working with a competitor and has a model in mind for the solution they need. Is it possible to reopen this prospect's mind to another possible solution? Yes, absolutely. It isn't easy. A few points to keep in mind:

- *Don't go negative.* Negative selling is not going to work in this situation. If the customer has a buying vision in mind, you are unlikely to create doubt by going negative. It is never a good idea in selling, and it is particularly counterproductive when the customer is already envisioning using the competitor's product.

- *Create doubt.* Create doubt in the customer's mind by offering a competing vision that provides more value. The additional value in your offer has to be tangible and quantifiable. Vague promises are not going to sway the buyer. Give him or her a challenge that her or she really has to stop and think about.

- *Run the numbers again.* Your competitive buying vision has to provide information that compels the customer to run the business case assumptions and financial justifications again. If you can't reach this stage, then it's unlikely that you'll be able to be taken seriously as a competitor on this deal.

CHAPTER 19

Being 1 Percent Better Is Enough

THE DIFFERENCE between winning and losing any sales deal you are working on is 1 percent.

Close your eyes, and think back for a moment to your first big order. That was a moment to savor, wasn't it? You probably crushed the competition, right? One question about that order: How much better were you than your competitors? After all, the customer had to have had a compelling reason to choose you. Were you 75 percent better than your competitors? 50 percent? 25 percent? 10 percent? Did it matter?

How about that big order you lost? Was the winning competitor 100 percent better than you? 50 percent? How about 5 percent better? Did it matter?

Yes, in both cases it mattered. (If the customer perceived your competitor to be more than 1 percent better than you then you probably were selling to an unqualified prospect. You don't want to waste time on prospects like that. Check out Chapter 30 to fix that problem.)

Customer decisions usually come down to the small stuff. You would like to believe that you have provided your prospects with a compelling and highly differentiated value proposition and that the decision to buy from you was not even a close one. But it doesn't work that way. In a globalized economy with increasing numbers of competitors in every category—and when the differences between products are narrowing, not growing—it becomes increasingly difficult for customers to differentiate between you and your competitors. If sellers increasingly all look alike to buyers, how big of a margin of incremental value do you really need to offer in order to win an order?

The difference between winning and losing a sale is a razor-thin margin of error: plus or minus 1 percent. You only have to be perceived to be 1 percent better than the alternative products or services your prospect is considering in order to win the order.

Before I explain how I arrived at the 1 percent, let's break it down with a couple of ground rules about competition and forecast probabilities.

First, in every sales situation you will have competition. Even if there are no other salespeople competing on a deal, you will still be competing against the dreaded no-decision. The customer always has the choice to decide not to decide. And the specter of that no-decision decision looms over every sales opportunity.

Second, when salespeople are forced to estimate the probability of winning, those estimates are nearly always inaccurate and generally worthless. We've all been in the position of racking our brains to come up with a justifiable probability of winning a particular order. Or perhaps your company uses a stage-based forecast methodology where the probability of winning a deal is assigned based on the particular stage a deal has reached. Just talking to a lead, qualified or not, is usually good for 10 percent. A first discovery call usually knocks the probability up to 25 percent. A submitted proposal, irrespective of its merits, usually merits a 75 percent chance of winning the deal. Isn't it ironic how the mere fact that a prospect hasn't yet kicked you out the door enables you to boast that your chance of winning the deal has increased?

Instead, think about the 1 Percent Strategy. If you are trying to take advantage of the Peak/End rule of selling, then you have to create peak experiences that are memorable to the customer. The question is how much more memorable? How much higher do your peak events have to be?

The 1 Percent Strategy means that in any competitive sales situation, the value you provide has to be perceived by the customer to be only 1 percent better than the alternatives in order for you to win the business. Rather than brainstorming a scheme to blow the customer away, just be the better alternative in the simple and somewhat mundane ways that most competitors overlook and that can often spell the difference between victory and defeat.

To gain an understanding of this, let's employ some simple math. (I was a history major, so simple math is all you are going to get.)

Here is Formula 1:

$$\text{Probability of winning the order} = \frac{100}{\text{Number of competitors}}$$

Up until the moment the customer makes a decision, your odds of winning that particular customer order is no better than 100 percent divided by the number of competitors in the deal. (Don't forget that the number of competitors must include the customer's ever-present option of no-decision.) How could you possibly justify a probability higher than this? Just because you are at the proposal stage of the sales process, do you think your odds of winning the business just got higher?

Imagine four evenly matched competitors lined up to run a 1,500-meter race around a track. If all four were neck and neck after 1,200 meters, would they each have a 75 percent chance of winning just because they got that far?

Here is Formula 2 for your winning sales strategy:

$$\text{Your probability of success} = \frac{100}{\text{Number of competitors} + 1}$$

In this case the +1 is not your date for the party but the incremental tangible and intangible value the prospect perceives that you bring to the table relative to your competition. Let's say a prospect is considering a major capital outlay on new manufacturing equipment and has received bids from three companies, including yours. Each proposal makes a clear and convincing case for the IRR and the value that the prospect will receive from the bidder. Using Formula 1, your odds of winning the business stand at 25 percent. Formula 2 says that you need only increase the prospect's perception of your value by 1 percent to win their business.

Let's say you are working on a big order and you have only one competitor. That means your odds of winning the deal stand at no better than 33 percent (the competitor has a 33 percent chance, and the no-decision decision has a 33 percent chance). Ultimately, the winner will be the seller who provides the incremental value through his selling to earn that last percentage point differential and become the 34 percent to the others' 33 percent and 33 percent.

That extra 1 percent lies in the peak experiences you created during the buying process. Think about the customer's evaluation process like mixing the ingredients to bake a cake. First, you put the wet ingredients into your mixing bowl. You turn on your mixer to blend those together, and then you add your sugar and flour bit by bit until everything is smoothly combined. And then at the end, you add dashes of favorite spices that make the ultimate difference in how the cake tastes.

Similarly, your prospects start their evaluation of your proposal by throwing into the mixing bowl the information they glean from your website and the content you provided as answers to their questions. After all that is mixed together, in go the insights and stories you provided along with your pricing. At the end, the prospects toss in their first perceptions and Peak/End experiences with you. These final additions—your incremental value—can make all the difference. Did you respond more quickly and completely to the prospects' questions? Did you consume less of their time in the buying process? Did you deliver value at each step of the sales process? Did you ask perceptive questions about the prospects' requirements? Did you provide a new insight into their business that helped them better understand those requirements? Did you make it easy to do business with you?

An extra 1 percent of value added at the right time can make a 100 percent difference.

CHAPTER 20

Making Your Selling Memorable

HOW DO YOU create memorable peak experiences for the customer? A variety of factors will influence how you approach this essential step in your selling. Your customer, the product or service you are selling, your personal sales strengths and style, your company, the size of the opportunity, and your customer's decision-making process will all influence how you create memorable sales interactions. However, aside from the tactics that you will employ to create a peak event during a sales interaction, some fundamental strategies should form the baseline of your selling efforts. In this chapter, I will discuss some of these strategies and how to use them in your selling to differentiate yourself from the other options the customer is evaluating.

But first remember that you have the ability to dictate and control your own success in sales. I came of age in selling in the computer industry when IBM still had an 80 percent market share. A lot of customers were just not going to buy from anyone but IBM. However, the rise of the Internet and the access it provides to information of all kinds to support decision making have changed the willingness of customers to consider a broader range of potential suppliers. Think about how the power of the brand-name product is rapidly diminishing across all industries. A study by Ernst & Young found that only 25 percent of the Americans surveyed said that brand loyalty had an impact on how they made purchase decisions. This creates opportunities for all sellers to compete for new business with customers who were previously closed to them.

Here are strategies to use Peak/End selling to your advantage:

Stop selling and start serving. Yes, you read that correctly. Stop selling— at least consciously. Now is the time to reorient your thinking about what you do on a daily basis. If your customer's objective is to gather the information in order to make informed decisions more quickly and at a lower cost, then it is your primary responsibility to make that happen. Being selfless and focused on the needs of the customer is an incredibly effective trust-building step.

Transition from seller to advisor. As you learn more about a customer's motivations and justifications for buying a product like yours, the composition of the information that you are providing will change. As customers move through their buying processes, they require less product content and more business insights. Whether based on the experiences of other customers, your industry expertise, third-party research, or some other source, you want your customers to rely on your business acumen to advise and guide them to a decision. Any insight that can help customers understand more fully how your product can be used to produce results that will meet or exceed their expectations can produce a peak event. Any insight that will help customers more completely understand the financial returns to be generated from using your product is also such an event.

Make it easy. Make it easy for customers to get necessary information from you. This is what buying and selling are all about. Too many companies get all bound up by their own rigid sales procedures and make their customers work too hard to get the information they need. Think about how you sell from the perspective of the customer. If you were a customer of your own company, what would you expect the buying experience to be like?

Deliver value. Deliver value on every single sales interaction with a customer. As mentioned in Chapter 12, every sales interaction with a customer has the potential to be the peak experience for them with you. It cannot be predicted in advance which step of the selling process will be the most important. Be respectful of the customer's time. Eliminate ad hoc sales calls, which, like check-in calls, provide no value to anyone. Remember that you are trying to maximize the customer's return on time invested (ROTI) in you.

Turn the customer into an internal advocate. There is a moment in a buying process when your primary points of customer contact morph into sellers themselves. That transformation is a peak experience. Once they have their buying vision firmly locked into place, they'll have a feeling of ownership because they worked with you to develop it. Now a good percentage of the time they have allocated to their buying process will be spent selling that vision to the internal resources that influence and ultimately approve the purchase decision. Part of your role is to give your customers the tools they need to be successful on your behalf. They need continuing access to the content, insights, and stories on which their buying vision sits.

Provide unconditional support. Salespeople usually think of support as a postsales event. But it applies to presales as well. At some point in virtually every sales cycle, there will be a hiccup. In the worst cases, even with supremely well-qualified prospects, the sales process can come to a screeching halt. At that point, the salesperson needs to put on a service hat. Similar to a support person working to resolve a customer problem as fast as possible, the salesperson must do whatever it takes to address the problem and start the process moving forward again. Remember, when it comes to support, customers' problems are always valid. They might not always be right. But from their perspective, a legitimate problem needs to be addressed immediately. Do whatever it takes to fix it. Receiving unconditional support is always a peak experience.

Accommodate the extraordinary. As salespeople, we have a natural tendency to want to slot customers into a niche that aligns with our own sales process. "This customer is in Industry B. I sell to all Industry B customers this way." The problem is that customers are not one-size-fits-all. And they can usually recognize when they run into a rigid sales process that conflicts with how they want to gather information. At that moment of recognition, do you default to, "I'm sorry, I'm afraid we can't do that." Or do you work with the customer to determine the information needed and brainstorm alternative methods for procuring it?

Sweat the small stuff. Who pays attention to the small stuff? Your customer does. I once had a colleague, Hal, who assiduously sent handwritten thank-you notes to every person he had had contact with in his selling. Once I went on a sales call with Hal to a customer he thought would soon close. The customer's desk had just a few papers on it. But on top of everything was a thank-you note from Hal. He won the order. Did his note make a difference? You tell me.

Invest in yourself. Salespeople have to invest the time and energies they have available for self-improvement on the knowledge-based sales skills like those I have covered in this book. Don't get me wrong. I believe it is important to allocate time to improve your activity-based skills such as how to make better cold calls, improve sales presentations, make more social connections, write a better proposal, craft a better subject line on an e-mail, ask for the order, and so on. The problem is that activity-based skills are all sales-centric; in and of themselves, they deliver minimal value to the customer. The power of knowledge-based skills is that they can convert intangible benefits to tangible value. Responsiveness can shorten the customer's buying process. This has a quantifiable value. Developing the domain expertise to provide business insights that help shape the customer's buying vision can result in a more productive solution that generates better business results. This has a quantifiable value. And it is very memorable.

PART IV

Growing Through Follow-Up

CHAPTER 21

The Simplest Strategy for Growth

THERE IS NO simpler or faster strategy to grow your sales than to effectively follow up your sales leads. I have worked with companies and salespeople that have doubled their sales in just a few short years merely by changing their procedures for following up their sales leads. It isn't a difficult task. For the most part, the skills required to do it well are those that we have already discussed so far in this book: creating positive first perceptions, being completely responsive, delivering maximum value, and creating peak events that are memorable to the customer.

But if follow-up is the key to sales growth, what is holding you back? According to an Insidesales.com study, 73 percent of sales leads are never contacted by a salesperson. I have never understood this reticence. You have a choice. You can generate qualified sales opportunities by talking with people who have reached out and expressed an interest in talking to you. Or you can make cold calls to people who haven't reached out and don't want to talk to you.

I recently read an article about the art of the follow-up. The author was making the case that we can all learn certain skills that will improve the effectiveness of our sales lead follow-up. It was hard to argue with his premise.

Unfortunately, that author put the cart before the horse. Certainly there are skills to be learned that, if regularly practiced, will improve the quality of your follow-up. However, there's a caveat that trips up many, if not most, sellers: Before you can practice the art of the follow-up, you actually have to pick up the phone and call the prospect.

The truth is that successful sales lead follow-up is as much about attitude as it is the art. In follow-up, attitude precedes art just as form follows function.

"These are bad leads. I can tell just by looking at them."

Really? How often have you said that? Or heard other salespeople make this claim?

I hate to say it, but I still hear salespeople say this as though they believe it. When so much has changed in how our customers initiate their buying processes—how they gather and evaluate the information that they need to make decisions and how they interact with vendors and their salespeople—surely you can't believe that you can accurately guess the potential value of a lead just by glancing at it. Besides, not only have customer behaviors changed, but selling has also changed. Much of what salespeople do to win orders today has evolved in its execution, if not its intent, from how things were 20 years ago.

Even today, in the face of the explosion of technology and information presaged by the growth of the Internet, some sales myths persist from earlier times. First among these is the belief held by many salespeople that "All marketing-generated leads are bad." This is followed closely by, "The only good lead is one I developed myself."

Which begs the question: What is a sales lead?

A sales lead is an inquiry. Many companies have deployed content marketing strategies to attract the interest of potential customers. They dangle content in front of visitors to their websites in the hope that they will register to download it. Some companies think that's a sales lead. It is not.

Yes, if you consider someone downloading a white paper from your website to be a lead, you will likely have bad leads. Referring to Figure 11–2 in Chapter 11, these customers are still in the Shopping Phase of their buying cycles. Customers enter your sales funnel when they are much deeper into their buying processes. At that moment, potential prospects want to know the answers to questions that they can't find on your website or else-where. At that point, they need you to answer a question. And, as you know from reading the first three parts of this book, the first seller with the answer wins!

Follow-up is a *live* conversation with the customer. An automatically generated e-mail in response to an inquiry is not follow-up. Unfortunately, many companies think that it is. Their attitude is, "OK, we can check off the follow-up box. We responded to the lead, and now let's make the customer reach out to us once more to show that he's really serious."

That attitude needs to change. Your sales procedures shouldn't be designed to force customers to work hard to get you to answer their questions. That will only drive them into the arms of your competitors.

Here are the building block traits of the necessary attitude for effective follow-up:

- *The Open Mind.* Sales leads are neither all bad nor all good. Not every good lead turns into a qualified sales opportunity for you. But you can't make that judgment before you engage with the prospect. So make the call first before you decide whether it is a good lead.

- *The Desire.* Why did you become a salesperson in the first place? It wasn't just for the money. You are always hungry for new business. If you're in sales, part of the attraction is the excitement of the process itself. If you're a salesperson and you lose that desire to follow up a sales lead and discover whether it has the potential to be your next big order, then perhaps it is time for a career change. On the other hand, if you're too successful and too busy with customers to take on new leads, and you can't be bothered to follow up, give the leads to those who will.

- *The Competitiveness.* You hate losing. Not only do you want to follow up a sales lead, but you absolutely, positively have to be the first seller to talk to the customer. You understand what is at stake.

You have the opportunity to create a positive perception and begin shaping the customer's buying vision if you get in first. You operate under the assumption that if you don't immediately follow up, your biggest competitor will.

■ *The Service Orientation.* I use the term "equivalence" to describe how salespeople should treat the follow-up. Ask yourself this question: If the tables were turned, how would you want a seller to follow up on your inquiry? If you were interested in a company's products and you submitted an inquiry, what would be your expectations for follow-up? You must have some expectations. After all, if you didn't expect someone from the company to get back to you, you wouldn't have taken the time to reach out to it. Now you can apply an equivalent expectation to your own follow-up efforts. Someone took the time to contact you. Reciprocate with equivalent interest.

In short, you have to care.

I remember searching online for pricing information on software that I wanted to use for my business. The vendor offered only two service options on its website: Professional (Individual) and Enterprise. Frustratingly, the company's website contained no pricing information on either option and no way to purchase the product. I filled in a web form requesting pricing information. Two weeks later, I received an e-mail response from a sales manager stating that if I wanted price information I would have to set up a phone call with her to go over my requirements. Two weeks. In the meantime, I had purchased an alternative solution.

Clearly they didn't care. To succeed in sales, you have to care about the customer. You have to care how your actions (or inaction) impact the customer's perception of you and your company. The first opportunity you get to demonstrate how you care is in how you follow up.

The art of follow-up is less important than the act of follow-up. Get in the game first. As a seller, you simply have to commit to take action—quickly. Put aside thoughts of technique until you take an action that would benefit from it. And then work on your craft.

CHAPTER 22

The No-Lead-Left-Behind Sales Process

EVERY SALESPERSON needs to employ a No-Lead-Left-Behind policy.

This means that you, a salesperson, have to embrace the attitude that a sales lead has value until it is proven otherwise and that the only way to quickly and accurately define the potential of that value is to reach out and engage with the customer making the inquiry.

It may be tempting to read this and tell yourself that lead follow-up isn't a problem for you. But a number of studies suggest otherwise. I believe that it is important for you to understand the magnitude of the problem because it ultimately will be up to you to fix. Management can put into place all the procedures it wants to improve follow-up, but until you buy into it, things aren't going to change.

The state of sales lead follow-up is not good. As referenced in the previous chapter, some studies found that, at the high end of the range, roughly 70 percent of sales leads are never contacted by a salesperson. On the low end of the range, seminal studies like the MIT Lead Response Management Study found that 37 percent of sales leads were never followed up. Personally, I think that anything above 0 percent is extremely problematic—and completely unnecessary. No matter which end of the statistical spectrum you subscribe to, the bottom line is that sales lead follow-up suffers from inattention and ineffectiveness.

Another key finding of the MIT Lead Response Management Study was that it is not enough to simply follow up. The effectiveness of follow-up is directly tied to how quickly it occurs. The study demonstrated that the longer you take to follow up, the less likely you are to actually contact the customer. The researchers found that salespersons are 21 times more likely to contact a customer if they call to follow up within five minutes of receiving the lead versus 30 minutes. In short, whatever priority the customer has placed on talking with you will begin to wane immediately after reaching out to you.

This means that the potential value of a lead begins to drop almost as soon as the customer sends it to you. The MIT study found that the average time to follow up a sales lead was 42 hours. If you were 21 times less likely to contact the lead if you waited 30 minutes to call versus 5 minutes, how many times less likely will it be that you can actually contact the customer if you wait the full 42 hours? As mentioned, I was a history major, so I'll leave it to you mathematicians to calculate the solution. But I can tell you this: The answer is going to look at lot like never.

One final point on this subject: Let's split the difference between the high and low end of the follow-up spectrum and agree that approximately 50 percent of sales leads are not appropriately followed up. Now consider the projection that $171 billion was spent in the United States on various forms of media to generate interest in products and services among potential customers. If salespeople preemptively deem 50 percent of the leads generated by those dollars unworthy of follow-up, then roughly $85.5 billion was essentially flushed down the drain due to sales inaction.

So what's new about that? Haven't salespeople always possessed an inherent skepticism about the value of marketing-generated leads? Yes. And there may have been a valid reason for this behavior in the past. But an in-bound sales lead today is a very different creature from the sales lead of the past, and it demands a different proactive response. Hence No Lead Left Behind.

First, sales leads today are not your daddy's sales leads.

A 2010 study showed that more than 90 percent of all B2B customers conduct some form of online research on a product or service before they engage with a salesperson. This means that most potential customers have initiated their buying process well before ever talking with a salesperson.

Prior to the widespread adoption of the Internet as a means to both promote and research a company's products, potential buyers had few sources of information about a company or its products. So-called bingo cards used to generate many sales leads. Bingo cards—aka reader inquiry cards—were postcards bound into the seam of a magazine that listed the names of the companies that were mentioned in the editorial or advertising in that issue. Readers circled the names of the companies whose products they were interested in learning more about, tore the postage-paid postcard out of the magazine, and dropped it in a mailbox. A fulfillment house processed the cards and passed the reader's name on to the relevant company.

The value of the bingo card leads was pretty low. Most came from people who were merely curious about a product or service, and without the Internet to easily supply this information they had to reach out to the company to learn more. In this environment, it was rarely worth the sales effort to sort through the 99 percent of the "leads" that were just tire kickers in an effort to find that 1 percent who might be qualified as a prospect. (A study of bingo card effectiveness reported in the *Journal of Direct Marketing* found that "Advertisers' response to requests for information via bingo cards tends to be very slow, if they respond at all.")

The situation has evolved for the better for both buyers and sellers. The Internet provides a low-cost, low-touch means for companies to deliver detailed information about their products and services to any interested party. As a result, the merely curious information seeker no longer has to reach out to a company and consume its sales time just to satisfy basic curiosity about a product or service. Today, your customers are doing their research and reaching out to sellers asking, "Sell to me, please." But salespeople continue to act as if all inbound sales leads were coming from bingo cards (or were contaminated with radioactive waste).

In fact, the Internet and the widespread acceptance of the basic compact of permission-based marketing between buyer and seller mean that information seekers who reach out to companies today are much more likely to be valid sales leads. (Please note that I am saying "leads," not "qualified prospects.") People who fill out a web form on a website know that they are giving that company permission to fill their inboxes with a carefully calibrated sequence of automatically generated e-mails that are designed to engage and sufficiently qualify their interest. Knowing what is in store for them (i.e., a call from a salesperson), most people don't casually fill out multiple web forms on a company's website unless they are prepared to engage with a salesperson.

As a result, the inbound leads that a company receives are from a different audience than that of 10, 15, or 20 years ago. These are valid leads from people who have done their homework and deserve a response by sales. Unfortunately, this doesn't happen as often as it should.

The mathematical logic behind sales lead follow-up is overwhelming. We have already established that I'm no math genius, except when it comes to calculating the size of an order and the commission earned on it. That is one of those skills you learn early in your sales career that will stick with you forever. The same is true of the math of sales lead follow-up. It's what I call the Immutable Multiplier Effect. If you keep your conversion percentage (leads to orders) level and double the number of sales leads you follow up, what happens? That's right. Your sales will increase proportionally to the number of sales leads that you followed up.

If you are looking for a way to increase your sales, this is the most obvious method. If you're hungry to succeed, or maybe just running behind on your quota, start digging into the leads. I had a client with three-quarters of the sales team underwater with quota. The CEO brought me in to help him figure out why they were struggling. It quickly became apparent that the salespeople weren't following up their leads. Most had made the decision that the leads they were receiving were worthless. Instead, they were risking significantly greater amounts of their time trying to prospect for new customers. Once they understood the multiplier effect, they began to treat their leads with respect and produce better results. Not everyone became a superstar, but everyone's sales increased.

Follow-up is on you. It's a process that only you can own and that every salesperson needs to master. Your managers can put metrics into place to measure it (and they should). But at the end of the day, you have to make it happen. The actions you take will spell the difference between converting a lead into a potential customer or having the opportunity passed to a competitor.

Commit to leaving no lead behind, and you'll soon be getting ahead.

CHAPTER 23

Standing Out by Following Up

GREAT FOLLOW-UP that makes you stand out is all about the process—on a personal level.

You may think that your company has a procedure for sales follow-up, but it probably doesn't. I have surveyed hundreds of companies about their sales processes in the past two years. I found that fewer than 20 percent have a written documented process for lead follow-up. Which means that the responsibility for figuring out how to effectively engage with customers is laid at the feet of the salesperson. It's your process. Speaking of which, exactly what is *your* process for following up sales leads?

For instance, exactly how long does it take you to follow up on a sales lead from the time you receive it until you talk to the customer? Granted, few salespeople have a concrete answer for this. But if you are trying to win the critical perception battle in your first contact with your customers, you need to know whether your process is helping or hindering that effort.

Do you have a written sales process that documents how you are going to follow up your sales leads? If your company doesn't have a well-defined and documented process, then you need to create one yourself. It's hard to set a standard for responsiveness without an explicit process.

What are salespeople supposed to do?

Given that you have so little time in which to impress customers, you have to stand out from your competitors from your first interaction with a new sales opportunity. Increasingly, customers are demanding that sales-people be more than just "account coordinators" who serve as traffic cops for the flow of information. They don't need a salesperson to hold their hands and walk them through their buying processes. As I have discussed throughout this book, customers must see the value you are delivering to their decision-making process. You need to be able to talk the talk and walk the walk.

This first interaction you will have with a customer often flows from follow-up. I have two prerequisites for effective follow-up that every sales-person should complete.

1. Know more about your product than the customer. Effective sales follow-up requires a baseline level of product and industry knowledge. This is not the follow-up of entry-level business development reps making outbound calls to visitors to their companies' websites who have registered to download a white paper and whose lead score has reached the point where it is deemed appropriate to call them. This is an actual follow-up to a sales lead, a potential qualified prospect who has come to you with a question. And to be effective, follow-up requires that you know at least as much about your product and its application as the customer knows.

That is not a very high bar to set, but it's important. Your objective should be to eliminate the get-backs in your selling. What's a get-back? Here's an example: "Well, Mr. Prospect, that is a great question. Unfortunately, I don't have the answer. I'll have to 'get-back' to you on that." No matter how well intentioned you are, a get-back wastes time and opens the door for your competitors. Get-backs are responsiveness killers. And deal killers.

2. Be ready with your killer questions. As a salesperson, you typically operate in one of two modes. The first is broadcast mode, and the second is receiving mode. Most salespeople are more comfortable in broadcast mode because if they are talking, the customer can't ask a question. They fear that if a customer asks a question, it will expose their lack of product knowledge. So they keep talking.

But the first proactive contact with a customer is not about communicating information. You don't enter your first follow-up contact with customers in broadcast mode. You are there to listen to them. To encourage them to talk about their requirements, you have to ask questions. It's most important for you to know the right questions to ask. Killer questions.

Killer questions reveal an intimate knowledge of the customer's business. They cut right to the heart of the requirements. A killer question isn't one of the routine, superficial questions that most salespeople ask their prospective customers. A killer question forces customers to stop and think before answering. You are asking them to reveal something about their requirements that they are not normally asked to share with a salesperson.

Customers will also pause because they are reappraising you. Customers tend to have a lowest-common-denominator opinion of salespeople. They don't expect much from them, and therefore they aren't disappointed when they don't get much from them. A killer question upsets that fractional calculation. Now customers will wonder why the competitors have not asked this same question. In fact, I call them "killer questions" because they have the impact of killing the customer's desire to talk with your competitors.

For example, in my business, I ask potential clients penetrating questions about their core sales processes and sales metrics that I know they aren't tracking but should be. When they hear the questions, they pause before answering because they are a little panicked—they suddenly realize what they have been overlooking.

Once you are prepared to effectively follow up, imagine what would happen if you conditioned your customers to expect an answer to their inquiries and questions within an hour? Or how about 30 minutes? Imagine how your customers' perceptions of the value you are providing to them would skyrocket once they knew they could count on you to help them make informed purchase decisions with less time invested on their part. Just think how your orders would grow.

The concept is so simple, and yet it seems that every day I encounter examples of bad sales follow-up that needlessly waste prospects' time because sellers appear to be completely clueless about the negative consequences of their actions. (In fact, a killer question I ask CEOs and VPs of Sales is whether they have ever calculated how many dollars' worth of sales opportunities they have lost because of poor follow-up.)

Let's face the hard truth: In sales, you are standing all by yourself on a lonely island. At the end of the day, achieving your quota is totally up to you. You have to decide how you are going to allocate your time to the various avenues available to you to achieve this. If you are provided leads but complain that you don't have enough prospects, then you need to reexamine your follow-up process.

Here are four essential strategies that any salesperson can easily employ to be the first with the answers, stand out from the competition, and maximize the conversion of inbound sales leads into orders.

1. Follow-up on 100 percent of inbound sales leads. In my book *Zero-Time Selling*, I described how every sales lead is like a scratch-off lottery ticket. You don't know what you have until you scratch the wax off the face of it. How many people buy a lottery ticket and then wait until the next day to see if they have a winner? None. Your sales leads should be treated the same way.

What this means is that every sales lead needs to be followed up. Make sure that all inbound sales leads are entered into your customer relations management (CRM) system as soon as they are received and that each one is assigned to a salesperson for immediate follow-up. Use your CRM system daily to check and make sure that 100 percent of your sales leads are being followed up.

2. Follow up all leads in less than 60 minutes. How much time should it take to follow up a lead? Less than you think. Research cited in the *Harvard Business Review* states that you are seven times more likely to qualify a lead if the follow-up occurs in less than an hour. Think how many more prospects will move into your pipeline if you respond to 100 percent of your leads in an hour or less.

Leads have a short shelf-life. Every minute that follow-up is delayed, the value of that lead drops. And if your competitors swoop in to provide the prospect with answers while you're sitting on your hands, then you are suddenly fighting for second place.

I worked with one client to streamline its sales lead follow-up process to reduce response time to inbound sales leads from 24 hours to 30 minutes. The immediate result was more qualified prospects in their pipeline. The medium-term result was a doubling of their sales with the same number of salespeople.

3. Provide complete answers quickly. As previously discussed, a sales lead is nothing more than a question. Being responsive to prospects means that you are providing complete answers to their questions in the least time possible. The best way to do this is to position your deepest product knowledge closest to the customer. It's not enough to be the first to respond. You must also be the first to answer the customer's questions. The first seller to respond to an inbound sales lead with the complete answer in zero time will build trust and credibility, dramatically increasing the chances of winning the order.

4. Measure, improve, and measure again. You must continually work to improve your sales lead follow-up process. As the old saying goes, "You can't improve what you don't measure." So keep it simple to start with and measure the following:

- How many sales leads do you receive each week?

- How long does it take to respond to each sales lead? (That's the time between when the lead is received and when a salesperson talks to the prospect for the first time.)

- What percentage of your inbound sales leads are converted into qualified prospects?

- What percentage of your inbound sales leads are converted into orders?

Set goals for these metrics, and then check each month to see whether you are achieving them. If you are, set more aggressive goals and fine-tune each element of your lead follow-up process to achieve the new goal. If you aren't meeting your goals, examine each element of your process in detail, and implement steps you can take to improve it. Then check your performance again in a month, and set even more aggressive but achievable goals.

PART V

Amp Up Your Prospecting

CHAPTER 24

To Cold Call or Not to Cold Call

To cold call, or not to cold call—that is the question:
Whether 'tis wiser in the mind to suffer
The slings and arrows of outrageous rejection
Or to take aim against a sea of prospects
By e-mail and Linking with them. To call, to fail—
No more—and by a fail to say we end
The heartache, and the thousand natural shocks
That sales is heir to.
(With deepest apologies to William Shakespeare!)

FEW SUBJECTS in sales today generate as much controversy as cold calling. There is a seemingly never-ending debate in sales circles over the relative and absolute merits of cold calling as a method for lead generation and prospect development. With the growing number and increasing sophistication of sales resources available to the average seller, it would seem strange that opinions among sales leaders and sales professionals could be so polarized on this subject.

On one side of this argument are the traditionalists, who believe that cold calling, even in today's information-rich economy, remains:

- An effective tactic for reaching new prospects.

- A productive use of a salesperson's limited selling time.

- An essential skill that every salesperson needs to master.

On the other side of the debate are the progressives, who believe that:

- Cold calls are unnecessary because a variety of tools enable a seller to connect and engage with prospects before the first call is made.

- Cold calling is an inefficient use of a salesperson's limited selling time.

- Contemporary sales skills, such as social selling, are more crucial to sales success than the elevator-pitch skills of cold calling.

Proponents on both sides of the debate tend to view this as an either/or proposition. It isn't. In fact, I am going to end the debate once and for all.

First, cold calling is not selling. Although it's often the responsibility of a salesperson, cold calling shouldn't be confused with selling. As you have learned in this book, selling is about helping customers get the information they need to make purchase decisions with the least investment of their time possible. Is there any part of that definition that sounds like cold calling? Nope. Selling is about providing answers that result in orders. Cold calling is about building interest in your product or service. Wait a second. Isn't building awareness and interest in your product the responsibility of marketing?

Hmm. Yes, it is.

If that's the case, then why on earth are you cold calling?

Well, you are cold calling only because your marketing department isn't doing a good enough job. Having a salesperson cold call a customer, someone who may never have heard of your company or product—whether over the phone, or in person out in the field—is an activity designed to create awareness and interest in your product. In other words, cold calling is just a form of advertising. The definition of advertising in *Merriam-Webster* is "the action of calling something to the attention of the public." Cold calling is a very personal, up-close, and mostly expensive form of advertising. And advertising is not the responsibility of sales.

How is marketing failing? They aren't generating enough quality sales leads to ensure that salespeople don't have to make cold calls. In most companies, there is a gap between the number of leads supplied by marketing and the number of leads sales requires to fill out its pipeline with well-qualified prospects. The utopian view of this situation is that marketing, through its activities, would reliably generate enough appropriate leads that a salesperson would never need to spend a single minute cold calling. You'd have more good leads than you'd have the time to handle. Unfortunately, this utopian vision of marketing fully living up to its responsibilities doesn't come to fruition in most companies. That leads to my final point, which resolves this argument once and for all.

Sometimes you just gotta do what you gotta do. You have no choice. If marketing can't generate enough leads to fill your funnel, then you need to do whatever it takes to make up that deficit. That means prospecting, cold calling, business development, whatever you feel comfortable calling it.

I have read the results of studies and listened to endless presentations about the changes taking place in how sellers and buyers are interacting. In general, the trends are reflected in the DemandGen and Genius.com study titled "Inside the Mind of the B2B Buyer." One of its key findings was that more than 80 percent of B2B customers/buyers said that, on their purchase transactions, they had initiated contact with the seller. Less than 20 percent said that they were contacted cold by the seller. In other words, 80 percent of buyers, at least in the B2B space, were making themselves aware of the products and services that they needed and then reaching out to the seller. And they largely accomplished this using content that they found online and that was created by . . . marketing. So maybe marketing isn't doing such a bad job after all.

Because if the study is correct, it means that all the arguing about cold calling boils down to finding the last 20 percent of the sales opportunities you need to meet your quota. Personally, I'm not convinced that 20 percent is an accurate reflection of the sales situation today. But even if the number is actually larger, it's beside the point. The key takeaway is that while cold calling's place in the sales world is changing, as long as the lead deficit exists, it's still an essential task for most salespeople.

A lead deficit is the percentage of your total required sales leads that you need to develop on your own through some form of prospecting. Using my 20 percent figure from the previous study, for example, if you meet 80 percent of your sales goal today from prospects that originated as marketing-generated sales leads, then you have a lead deficit of 20 percent. The question then becomes what actions must you take to find the remaining 20 percent of the sales opportunities you need to make your quota? You will find them from proactive sales prospecting (i.e., cold calling).

Let's face facts here: In sales, your job boils down to doing whatever hard work is required to meet your goals. Whenever there is a gap between the number of qualified prospects required to reliably meet your goal and the number of qualified prospects in your pipeline generated from marketing activities—and there will almost always be a gap—it has to be filled in by prospect activity generated by you. This means fulfilling your responsibility as a salesperson to do what it takes to meet and exceed your assigned goal. If this means spending a portion of every day following a disciplined prospecting process (e.g., doing some research to pick targets, making connections online, getting on the phone, or going out and making calls), then that is what has to be done.

In the grand scheme of selling, is it desirable for salespeople to devote a significant portion of their time to cold calling? Absolutely not. It is not the most productive use of a salesperson's time.

On the other hand, when you have a lead deficit to make up, cold calling is absolutely necessary. And you'd better know how to do it and do it well.

CHAPTER 25

Doing What It Takes to Succeed

THE NEED FOR salespeople to proactively prospect for new sales opportunities (such as cold calling) is not going away any time soon. Certainly, the lead deficit discussed in the previous chapter will continue to shrink as more effective methods of engaging with potential customers are developed. But the lead deficit is not going to zero.

When I began my sales career, the Internet didn't exist, and I was responsible for generating 100 percent of the sales leads I needed to meet my quota. I was out in the field, trawling door to door through business parks, making as many as 50 cold calls in a day.

If my lead deficit then stood at 100 percent, these days it is somewhere between 10 percent and 20 percent. That gap is shrinking for most salespeople, but that doesn't portend an end to the need for proactive prospecting because the deficit is unlikely to ever be completely erased. Like it or not, you will always need to develop and implement your own plan for prospecting.

One of the primary reasons that salespeople have a hard time sticking with the discipline of prospecting is that they are forced to use a process that doesn't align with their sales strengths. Human nature dictates that people will avoid discomfort—and salespeople are especially adept at avoiding activities that make them feel uncomfortable. Prospecting is not a one-size-fits-all activity. A little experimentation is required to find the approach that best suits your personality, your skills, and the goals you need to achieve.

To determine the prospecting strategy that will work best for you, ask yourself the following questions.

Question 1: How much prospecting must I do? To begin, you need to quantify the challenge you face. How many leads do you need? Be specific. Start with your quota and work backward. Look at your sales history, and calculate your close ratio over the prior 12 months. What percentage of your sales opportunities did you convert into orders? Don't inflate this number. It's important to be accurate and honest with yourself. Once you have your close ratio in hand, use that to calculate how many prospects you will need in order to meet your quota. The last step is to estimate what percentage of those leads will flow in from marketing activities and what percentage you will need to develop through your own efforts.

The percentage of leads that you have to develop—the lead deficit you need to make up—will give you a pretty good estimate of how much time you must devote to prospecting. Having this information in hand will let you determine whether cold calling or some other prospecting activity is the optimal strategy to achieve your prospecting goals.

A rule of thumb that I suggest to my clients is that the percentage of time that a salesperson needs to devote to prospecting is approximately equal to the percentage of the lead deficit she needs to fill. For instance, if you are a new salesperson, your lead deficit might stand at 100 percent, in which case you will need to spend 100 percent of your time on prospecting until it begins to shrink. An experienced and established salesperson might have a 30 percent lead deficit. She will probably fill two-thirds of that deficit with repeat business and referrals, leaving a 10 percent gap. That salesperson would then need to spend about 10 percent of her time on prospecting.

Question 2: What am I good at doing? It's essential to align your prospecting activities with your sales strengths. This may seem obvious, but I work with a lot of companies that have rigid sales procedures that fail to take advantage of the strengths of their individual salespeople.

In fact, not everyone has to be good at all forms of prospecting. Take cold calling. Success in cold calling, or the lack thereof, can be due as much to salespersons' temperaments as their skills. And no amount of training can change that. I worked with a great salesperson at one company who was painfully shy. He was not going to pick up the phone and cold call a potential customer. He was skilled at using referrals to build his pipeline. Fortunately, he worked for a manager who showed flexibility in letting his people determine how they could best meet the challenge of prospecting.

Some people are comfortable with cold calling. Some are not. Others might be stronger in creating e-mails that get noticed. Or perhaps they are adept at connecting through LinkedIn. Maybe they have created a strong industry presence through a blog or speaking at conference. Or perhaps they are really strong at tapping customers for referrals.

The point is to identify a method that will work for you consistently and put it to use every day. Prospecting is a skill that improves with practice. In his book *Talent Is Overrated*, Geoffrey Colvin describes research demonstrating that individuals who are successful in a particular endeavor are not naturally gifted or innately skilled in that field. Instead, these experts are skilled at consistently practicing their craft at high levels and at improving their performance by closely monitoring and learning from their past performance. This discipline, known as "deliberate practice," has been popularized with the shorthand saying that it takes 10,000 hours of deliberate practice to master any skill.

What this means is that great salespeople are not born that way. It takes an investment of time over a long period to become really expert at prospecting. Choose the specific skills that you want to become expert in, and start practicing them on customers.

Question 3: What prospecting activity is the most effective use of my sales time? The ultimate decision about which method to employ should depend on which one gives you the best return on the time you invest in it. This means that you have to measure your results against the time you spend on prospecting. You have to track the actual amount of time that you spend on prospecting, and the number of leads and qualified sales opportunities you generated during that time.

Let's say that you have a 20 percent lead deficit to fill, but it requires 50 percent of your available selling time to develop the required number of sales leads. You have a problem. You either need to change the prospecting method you are using, or you need some coaching and guidance on how to improve what you're doing. If you have to make 50 phone calls to develop one new lead while John, sitting in the cubicle next to you, develops five new leads from 50 phone calls, then you need to ask for help. Shadow John and listen to him make his calls. Have John or your sales manager listen to you make calls and provide some feedback. (Remember that a crucial part of deliberate practice is learning from past performance to improve future performance.)

Prospecting, as performed by salespeople, is entrepreneurial. If a company employs you, you should consider your territory to be a franchise. Your employer is the franchisor, and you are the franchisee with the sales rights within a certain territory. You are the owner of your territory of potential customers, no matter how that territory is defined. And, just as in standard franchising agreements, if you, as the franchisee, do not invest the resources to deliver on the potential within your territory, then the franchisor can terminate your franchise and replace you with another entrepreneur.

It's up to you as the franchise owner to do whatever it takes to build a profitable business in your territory.

Small business owners commonly face this issue. They may have a marketing budget, but if that doesn't create enough leads, what are they going to do? Go out of business? Of course not! Maybe the weak-willed ones would give up and throw in the towel. But most entrepreneurs are more tough-minded than that. They will steel themselves and go out and undertake the activities necessary to generate sales leads. That could mean going door to door or joining the local chamber of commerce. It could mean attending networking events or researching a list of local prospects and then committing to making a certain number of cold calls every day before 9 A.M. They might not like doing these activities, but sometimes you just gotta do what you gotta do.

And so it is with you. Start your prospecting with the activities that are best aligned with your strongest capabilities. But if those activities aren't generating enough leads, then you have to try something else—even if it means picking up the phone and making cold calls. (As Shakespeare said, "Ay, there's the rub.")

CHAPTER 26

Sell More
The Difference Between Activity and Prospecting

I ONCE READ an article about what a salesperson could do to increase sales. The title was something catchy like "A Thousand and One Tips to Increase Sales." It was hard to argue with the premise. All salespeople can use good advice about how to increase their sales. It's the reason that I continue to read everything I can about selling. There is always something new to learn.

In this case, this author's useful quick tips were all about creating more sales activity. He was asking the question, "What should you do if you can't get potential customers, raw sales leads, to engage?" His recommended steps were intended to create a flurry of sales activity around raw prospects to stimulate engagement, initiate their own buying process, and move forward with the seller.

But is selling the same as sales activity? And if prospects are not yet fully committed to their buying processes, are random sales activities the most effective way to get them engaged?

Arte, a salesperson who once worked for me, was responsible for a large geographic territory. His lead deficit was normally about 50 percent, which meant that a good portion of his sales time was consumed by prospecting. One day he came into my office and announced that he had invented his own method of prospecting that he called SWARM. The acronym stood for Surround With Activity to Regain Momentum. His idea was to envelop his potential prospects in a constant swarm of sales activities such as phone calls, visits, e-mails, voice messages, invitations to webinars and seminars, and product demonstrations in the hope that eventually something would stick.

How'd that work for Arte? Not well. But he got high marks for creativity!

Unfortunately, many salespeople fall into this trap. How many times are you able to contact one of the names on your list on the first attempt? The percentage is fairly small. Or maybe you get through, but contacts tell you to call back in a couple months when they might be interested. This happens all the time. Rarely is the correct response to bombard the prospect with trivial, time-wasting communications and requests.

Sales managers and sales professionals often ask me: "If you had to choose one piece of advice to give me about how to grow sales, what would it be?" My standard answer is, "*Sell* more."

I like to illustrate the meaning of "*sell* more" with a parable about Eckstein, a salesperson for a typical medium-sized business. (Eckstein is a composite drawn from the stories of numerous salespeople I have helped over the years.) Eckstein always had an excuse for everything, including why he would always almost make his numbers but never quite get there. His boss was at a loss, so he summoned me, the sales expert, to analyze the problem.

Observing Eckstein in action was to see a typical salesperson at work. On the surface, it looked as though he was taking the right steps to succeed, and he seemed happy in his work. But something was holding him back from taking his productivity to the next level.

That something was that Eckstein had a problem distinguishing between enough and more. He was like most salespeople in that regard. He always thought he was doing enough to make his numbers and that if everyone else just did their jobs, then he would make his quota. It never occurred to him that the key to unlocking his success was doing more.

If you don't have enough prospects, then *sell* more.

The emphasis is on the *sell* not the more.

It's not about engaging in random sales activity, which is what gets salespeople like Eckstein stuck into the hole. To *sell* more means to fill your prospecting time with intelligent, productive, creative, and responsive sales actions that set you apart from your competitors and motivate potential customers to learn more.

What are the goals and desired outcomes of your prospecting activities? The prospecting call—be it a voice call, door knock, networking event, or e-mail—is the same as a regular sales call. Every contact has to be planned. On the very first prospecting contact, your plan has to answer the following questions:

- What do I want to accomplish in this call?

- What do I want the outcome of the call to be in terms of the next steps that the customer will take (such as scheduling a discovery call to learn enough about customers' requirements to qualify or disqualify them as prospects)?

Here are additional ways to *sell* more:

- *Prospect with existing customers to assess whether they have new requirements for your products and services.* The goal is to identify a potential need for additional products. The desired outcome is a meeting to explore a customer's potential requirements.

- *Call existing customers for referrals.* The goal is to get the customer's agreement to provide two referrals. The desired outcome is the customer committing to provide those names to you within two days.

- *Go to a networking event.* The goal is to make contact with five people whose companies may have a need for your product. The desired outcome is scheduled follow-up meetings with at least three of the five people you met.

- *Ask a contact on LinkedIn for an introduction to a mutual connection.*
The goal is for your contact to make the introduction within 24
hours. (Do this only with people you actually know.)

After exhausting all these resources, if you still have a lead deficit, then
you can go out and make some cold calls. But only after you have performed the necessary research and crafted a great killer question.

In my first professional sales job out of college, in the pre-Internet
dark ages, I was selling big computers. I had a 100 percent lead deficit.
Every day at 8 A.M., when my sales manager would kick me out of the
office, I ventured forth to make many, many cold calls in my territory. I
have to admit it didn't come naturally to me, so I developed another
approach. Rather than being a generalist, I decided to specialize in selling
to a specific vertical: the construction market. This way I could develop
an expertise that gave me something concrete to differentiate me. I did
not cold call the construction companies in my territory (and there were
hundreds of them), but rather I hosted a weekly educational seminar in
our branch office for a limited number of construction companies. The
program—held every Wednesday—would include a demonstration of
our construction management system, and customers seemed to prefer
the group setting to dealing with a salesperson one on one. I found potential prospects in business directories, and every Thursday would mail out
ten postcards with a handwritten invitation. Then I'd follow up twice:
first on Monday morning and again on the morning of the seminar.
Within months I had a strong, constantly renewing pipeline—and I was
killing my numbers! After a year, I was getting two-thirds of my sales from
existing accounts and referrals. But every Thursday, I was still sending out
ten postcards, and every Wednesday I was playing host to new prospects
(usually one or two per week).

Although it is important to fill every hour with selling, it is more
important to do it wisely. Persistently. Creatively.

Your prospecting must have a purpose. Keep in mind the customers'
objective: to gather the information or data required to make an

informed purchase decision with the least investment of their time possible. This is not to say that customers won't spend the appropriate time to purchase a product or service. They just don't want to invest a minute more than they have to.

The winning salesperson is usually the one who knows how to make that happen—and it often starts with how you prospect.

Sell more. Win more orders. Simple.

CHAPTER 27

Being Worth
a Second Call

VERY EARLY IN my sales career, I made a cold call on the CEO of a large homebuilder in my territory. I was selling construction management systems for a major computer company. Freshly trained in sales and computers, shoes shined, and red power tie straightened, I was a newly minted sales rep ready to go out and conquer. I marched into the lobby and up to the receptionist's desk and asked to see the CEO, fully expecting to be rebuffed. So I was completely taken aback when the CEO, Bill, came into the lobby, shook my hand, and escorted me back to his office.

Bill was very polite and completely old-school, with silver hair, a nice tan, and an expensive three-piece suit. His office was empty except for his massive wooden desk with a phone on it. He motioned for me to sit down opposite him and asked for my business card. He took it, slowly turning it in his hands, examining it back and front, and laid it on the desk in front of him. "So, Andy, what can I do for you?"

I took a deep breath and launched into my pitch, just as I'd been trained to do. He let me talk for a minute, and then he raised his hand for me to stop. He opened a drawer in his desk and pulled out a two-inch high stack of business cards bound with a rubber band. "These are all the computer salespeople that have been by my office in the last year." He spread the cards across the top of his desk. There were dozens of cards from nearly every competitor I could think of. "Tell me, how are you different or better than any of those folks?"

The answer was that I wasn't.

When you're prospecting for new customers, getting the first calls are relatively simple. Once your plan and process are in place, following them is simply a matter of execution. The hard part is getting the second call (which in reality is oftentimes the first sales call), which signifies that the customer is preparing to initiate his buying process. Compare self-developed sales leads with marketing-developed sales leads: Marketing-developed prospects have invested in the buying process prior to contacting your company. They have identified a need for change in their business. They have developed at least a broad set of requirements for the change. They have investigated potential solutions and have used the Internet and social media to research your product and others like it. And, they have made some preliminary decisions about which suppliers to talk to and which to exclude. With this type of sales lead, the first call with a salesperson is very different from an initial prospecting call. Preeducated marketing leads have questions that need to be answered and expectations for the information they need to receive in order to move forward with their buying process.

The first call with self-developed leads is very different: Usually the customers have little to no developed need or interest in a change. Nor have they initiated a buying process or researched potential vendors. When you contact those customers for the first time, they may answer the phone or spend a few minutes with you for no other reason than a little natural curiosity. Good businesspeople want to keep abreast of what is happening in their fields. So this customer may be willing to invest a couple of minutes in you with no expectation of a return, just on the off chance they can learn something.

This is the perfect illustration of the time exchange that is at the heart of all selling. Customers give you some of their time, and what are you giving them in return? How are you going to earn more selling time, in the form of a second call, with the customer?

I recommend a method I call "Story-Question-Listen." In a prospecting call, you are going to use a story, a question, and your ears to earn the all-important second call with a customer.

I learned later that Bill talked to nearly 50 salespeople just like me every year. Fifty salespeople were given an opportunity to speak directly with the CEO on their first calls. Bill had simplified the task for every salesperson. There were no layers to go through, no BANT (budget, authority, need, time frame) qualification to process because they were talking to the ultimate decision maker. And yet, no seller had ever gotten past the first call with Bill.

Why? Because Bill was simply waiting for someone to give him a compelling reason to consider making a change. That reason was not going to be a new feature or its associated benefits. He was patiently waiting for a salesperson to deliver value in the form of a compelling question or a unique business insight that would move him to invest his time and money in a new system. In short, he was waiting for a salesperson to step up and differentiate himself from the crowd of companies selling similar products.

Story-Question-Listen. Customers can talk to a hundred salespeople whose products can do exactly what yours does. Why should they spend more time with you?

Here are five easy steps to catch fire using the Story-Question-Listen method with potential leads while prospecting:

1. Warm up your cold calls. There is little reason for a salesperson to make a completely cold call. Whenever possible, before your first personal interaction, use a warm-up touch to engage the customer. For example, if you have a list of names that you are planning to call, first send them an introductory e-mail that contains a single insight about their business. This insight should be brief but of sufficient value to pique the customer's interest. It could be your killer question. It could be summary research findings about the value customers realized from using products like yours, the abstract of a case study about a customer, or even a customer testimonial. It could simply be an, "Are you aware . . . ?" question. "Are you aware that independent research has found that companies like yours that use products like mine are growing 25 percent faster than those who don't?" And then end the warm-up touch by stating that you are going to contact them at a specific date and time.

In addition to giving customers a reason to invest their time to talk with you, there is another important reason why you should do a warm-up touch prior to contacting a potential lead. This is to give customers the impetus to start their research on you before you contact them. The extent to which they are motivated to prepare for your first call indicates something about their level of interest. It also means that more ground can be covered during that session. If you have carefully targeted the companies you are warming up, this should increase your odds of getting that second meeting.

2. Tell a very short sales story. When you're prospecting, the customer is, at best, in the awareness stage of the buying process. At this point the customer—the potential lead—has one question for you: "What do you do?" Illustrate your answer with a succinct (30-second-or-less) sales story about one of your current customers, why the company chose you, and how it is using your product. (In Part VII, I get into detail about how to create these powerful stories.) The purpose of this story is to answer buyers' questions in such a way that they can begin to envision themselves using your product. In essence, the customer will take a mental test drive of your product during your first interaction. They will also hear some third-party validation for your product, an indirect testimonial from your customer. This is a powerful step from which the lead can form a positive perception of you.

3. Ask buyers their most important question. In Chapter 23, I introduced you to the notion of the killer question. Every buyer has one or two top-of-mind business questions during the awareness and interest stages of the buying process. In the case of the sales-developed lead, chances are that the customer is just entering the awareness and interest stages of that process. The killer question is a trigger for customer concern. It suggests to customers that they could be missing some key information about their own business. This level of insight is a trust and credibility builder. You should know from your own experience what the killer questions are for the type of companies or individuals that you are prospecting. If not, ask your peers or your manager. Follow up on the story you told by asking one of these important questions. This will show the customer that you have some insight and understanding of his business.

4. Stop and listen. This is powerful. Now that you've told your story and asked a killer question, you are waiting for the lead to tell you something that is important to him. If his reply contains inside information about his business, then you've made real progress. For instance, suppose the lead responds to your killer question by saying, "Yes, we're having a problem scaling this part of our production process, and we missed our forecast by 5 percent last year. How could your system help us fix that?" Now you are closer to having a lead that you can qualify.

5. Ask for one small commitment for immediate action. The next step is getting a commitment from the buyer. It's best to ask for a small commitment unless you are absolutely convinced that he is prepared to jump into a buying process after just one interaction with you. Make your request a small one—something the buyer can agree to without further thought. Perhaps you want to send him a case study about a problem he mentioned. Get a commitment for a phone call to review it with him. Build the interest and curiosity one step at a time.

What you just did in a very short time was (1) establish credibility with the customer by demonstrating a deep understanding of a main concern, (2) create more trust and credibility through the short story about the benefits that another firm received by working with you to answer the same question, and (3) gave the customer permission to open up and tell you his priorities.

These five simple steps will provide what you need to begin building a relationship with a potential customer. Building credibility and trust is not easy. Great salespeople make it look easy, but it often remains elusive even to the most experienced sales professionals. Practice makes perfect, however. The more you use this process or your own version of it, the more effective you will be in building a quick bond with your customers.

The lesson that I learned from Bill continues to grow in relevance for salespeople, both new and experienced. Today more than ever, how you sell is as important as what you sell to create value, build trust, and differentiate yourself from your competition. Bill had looked at the universe of product offerings that addressed his needs, and yet he had never gone past the first call with a seller. It isn't enough to show up at prospects' offices and expect them to fall in love with your product or service based solely on its features and benefits. Another thing about prospecting: It's not just a numbers game. You could make a million cold calls, but if you don't give your prospects a reason to invest their time in you, then you are never going to earn their business.

A little over a year later, I went to see Bill again. I was a bit wiser and more experienced. We began all over again, but this time there was a different outcome. Score!

CHAPTER 28

Practicing Value-Based Persistence

ANYONE WHO has ever sold for a living has encountered the following situation. You're talking for the first time to Larry, a decision maker at ACME Tech, a company that you feel could potentially be a fit for your product or service. But before you get two words out of your mouth, Larry shuts you down with either:

- "We already have a supplier," or

- "We're not in the market right now," or

- "We're not interested."

Or perhaps all three. Many sales leaders would have you believe that this response is merely an objection that can be overcome with the appropriate salesmanship. Not interested? No problem. Not in the market? No problem. Already have a supplier? No problem. Just sell harder.

Well, actually, there is a problem: the reluctance of salespeople to walk away from a potential sales opportunity. Statements of disinterest from customers are usually statements of fact, not objections. There are always exceptions to the rule, but in general people mean what they say.

In my consulting and speaking work, salespeople frequently ask me, "What should I do when people say they're not interested?" For my response, I harken back to my first boss in sales, Ray. He had the best and simplest answer to this question: "Go find someone who is."

We live and sell in a big world. There are lots of potential customers out there. Many will find you. Some you'll have to go find. Those who you find will be in varying states of readiness. Most won't be worth waiting for. Some will be, but they will have to be cultivated.

In those cases, you have to exercise some persistence. Persistence is a valuable characteristic to have when you're a salesperson. Persistence is about refusing to give up even in the face of adversity. And, as we all know, there can be a lot of adversity in selling. But persistence in itself has no value to your customers or to you. It must be applied correctly. Otherwise it can be perceived as annoying and time-wasting by your prospects, thereby dooming any chance you have to earn their trust and their business in the future.

The key is to learn how to be persistent without being a pest.

For that I recommend a process called Value-Based Persistence (VBP). Value-Based Persistence is a process any seller can use to effectively follow up and stay in touch with a customer until the timeframe for your sales cycle and her buying cycle are in alignment. Essentially, VBP is a form of scheduled responsiveness. It's the methodical delivery of carefully curated content over a defined period of time that is designed to move the potential customer to engage in a buying process.

It's important to know when to implement a VBP campaign for a potential customer. It's not automatically triggered when you run into resistance on an initial sales call. You have to be disciplined and analytical about it.

In fact, you need to ask yourself two tough self-directed qualifying questions and be sure to give yourself completely honest answers.

- *Self-Directed Question 1: Is this customer a great fit for our product or service?* Not a good fit, but a great fit. Does she fit the profile your company has established for the target customer for your product? This is prequalification before the customer begins the buying process.

- *Self-Directed Question 2: Is the solution I'm selling clearly superior to the alternatives the customer is already using or could acquire in the near term?* Set aside your corporate loyalty for a minute, and answer honestly.

In sum, you are answering the question, "Should I persist?"

There is no obvious answer to this question. Salespeople want to be convinced of the superiority of the solutions they sell, but the hard truth is that their solutions aren't always superior. Some products are better suited for some customers than for others.

Therefore, you have to be absolutely honest with your answers. Simply put, are you a better fit with the prospect's requirements than the other guys? Do you provide more value than a competitive solution? In similar situations, with similar customers, have you reliably beaten the competition? And have your customers been totally satisfied with the solutions you have provided?

There is a real downside to answering the questions incorrectly. You risk investing your most precious and limited resource—your time—pursuing a customer who will never buy from you. Think of all the other sales opportunities you will have to forego in order to work on this one. That is a big bet.

Let's ask the question again: Are you absolutely, positively the best solution for this customer? If the answer is no, then you need to just walk away. Other potential customers will be out there who will be better fits for your product. If the answer is yes, then you can proceed with your VBP campaign.

Many salespeople have a problem maintaining a balanced approach to persistent follow-up. You want to stay in touch with your prospects, but you don't want impose a constant full-court press on them. Remember that you are nurturing your relationship with prospects until their timing is right. You want to stay in communication, but prospects will continue to take your calls or respond to your e-mail only if you take pains to ensure that each communication delivers something of value to them. That means the information you provide has to serve a specific purpose, it has to have impact, and it has to respect the customer's time and yours.

Here are four simple steps to implement Value-Based Persistence in your selling:

1. Identify and gather all the critical pieces of information that your prospect requires to make an informed decision to purchase your product or service. Don't guess. Make a list of all the essential data that can be presented to or reviewed independently by the prospect. White papers, case studies, media coverage, product announcements, testimonials, webinars, videos, and seminars are just a few examples of the kinds of information that can deliver value to the customer.

2. Review each item on the list for its quantifiable value. Don't guess or assume that an item on the list will deliver value. Write down what the value is. What questions does it answer? What context does it create or insight does it provide for the prospect? Can the prospect use this content to learn something essential about how the prospect would use your product? Does it provide insight that illuminates the quantifiable value the customer could realize from using your product? Or does the information help the customer to make a better decision?

   Keep in mind that the information you provide as part of VBP has to distinguish you from your competition or the entrenched supplier. The customer doesn't want to hear that you are just as good as the other guys. If you are just one more mindless seller of a me-too product, then the customer won't have time for you. Give prospects a reason to engage with you and to listen to you.

3. Develop a delivery schedule to provide the information to the customer. You don't want to deliver the information all at once, of course. Because you know the chronology in which the information will be useful in the prospect's information gathering, create a schedule for delivering it and enter it into your CRM system. Use scheduled reminders from your CRM system or calendar to stay in sync with the customer.

4. Use intelligent tools to help deliver content to your prospect. Don't rely just on e-mails or phone calls to provide the information to the customer. Look at new collaborative sales engagement tools that enable you to create private information collections for your prospects, who will then receive e-mail notifications when you add additional content to their collections. These tools also provide analytics that enable you to track the customer's engagement with your content. For instance, you can learn which content customers viewed and how much time they spent on a particular page.

Then be persistent. If you create value for the buyer, you will eventually be given the opportunity to get in the door. It may take weeks or months. I've sold some multimillion-dollar deals that took years to mature to the point where the customer was ready to move forward. But when that day arrived, I had, to a large degree, already presold the customer on my solution. By using Value-Based Persistence, my odds of winning that order were substantially better than anyone else's.

PART VI

Qualification:
Doing More
with Less

CHAPTER 29

Are You Selling to the Right Customers?

IN MY EXPERIENCE, the biggest differentiator between salespeople who consistently achieve quota and those who struggle lies in how they use their time. I am not talking about time in general. I am specifically referring to selling time, the time spent on planning and executing sales interactions with customers. Top salespeople earn a higher return on their selling time. They achieve this by being more disciplined about selling to the right customers. Top sellers don't waste their limited selling time on potential sales opportunities with customers who are not absolutely qualified to buy what they are selling.

If you are not consistently hitting your targets, then an important question to ask yourself is, "Am I selling to the right customers?"

In this part of the book, I am going to give you a foolproof method for qualifying sales opportunities. Before I get to that, I want to make sure that you understand how effective qualification (or lack thereof) can impact your sales results.

Qualifying a sales opportunity is a binary event. A customer is either qualified or not. An opportunity cannot be mostly qualified. Or sort of qualified, as in "We can do about 70 percent of what this customer needs." I can't count the number of times I have heard a salesperson say this in a sales meeting. It is said with the conviction that somehow meeting only a fraction of the customer's requirements is a positive outcome. Selling to mostly qualified prospects is not a formula for winning an order.

What drives poor qualification? And why is it a problem for so many salespeople?

The root of bad qualifying is pressure—both self-imposed and from managers—for salespeople to demonstrate that they have a sizable pipeline of sales opportunities. Sales managers and, by extension, salespeople have an unhealthy preoccupation with the size of their pipelines. The quantity of names in a salesperson's sales pipeline is a lazy metric to assess the status of your sales efforts. It stands to reason that, if you are not so discriminating in qualifying potential sales opportunities, you will have more names in your pipeline. But at that point who is fooling whom?

The size of a pipeline doesn't tell anything about the likelihood of any of those deals turning into orders. In fact, the preoccupation with quantity over quality creates the conditions in which salespeople end up squandering their precious selling time with unqualified prospects and, as a result, creating greater uncertainty about their results.

Obviously, it's easier to fill a pipeline with mostly qualified sales opportunities than with qualified ones if you are less discriminating about the quality of your customers. But this sales behavior, if left uncorrected, leads to what I call a "vicious sales cycle" that will have a negative impact on your ability to achieve your sales goals.

You are undoubtedly familiar with the concept of a vicious cycle—a self-perpetuating series of negative events. A vicious sales cycle is a self-perpetuating series of negative sales behaviors. Once you are trapped in a vicious sales cycle, it's extremely difficult to free yourself from its clutches.

The first step in a vicious sales cycle is chronically poor sales qualification, such as admitting mostly qualified customers into your pipeline. From the beginning, the odds that they will buy from you are pretty low. But they are willing to talk with you, and salespeople have a weakness for customers who are willing to spend time with them—even if those customers don't intend to buy from them. And once having invested a certain amount of time in a sales opportunity, a salesperson will begin to have an emotional stake in it, putting on blinders and ignoring the obvious signs that the customer is really not interested.

Do you find yourself having to defend your pipeline in sales meetings? Do you struggle to explain to your manager or your peers exactly why a particular customer is going to buy from you? If so, then you may have fallen into a vicious sales cycle.

It starts with wasting your limited selling time with poorly qualified prospects who will likely not buy from you. You fall behind in your goals. You start getting a little desperate. The solution that comes to mind is that you need more opportunities to sell. So you lower your qualification standards ever further and jump at any potential sales opportunity you find and talk to any customer who will give you the time of day, all in a futile effort to make up lost ground. You waste more selling time on unproductive prospects that come to nothing. And you fall further and further behind. A vicious sales cycle indeed.

Breaking out of a vicious sales cycle requires that you take actions that may seem counterintuitive. You have to become more disciplined about customer qualification, not less so.

First, invest more time up front to ensure that the customer is absolutely qualified to buy precisely what you are selling. Unqualified prospects in your pipeline are exactly the same as having no prospects in your pipeline. Right? There is no chance you are going to win an order from either one of them. So why invest even one second of your time on them?

Second, qualify quickly. The initial qualification of a sales opportunity should not be an extended process. The goal is to convert shoppers into buyers and quickly shift the customer from a process of discovery to one of intent.

Third, review every name in your existing pipeline and disqualify the opportunities that aren't real. In *Zero-Time Selling*, I talked about the need to disqualify the losers, which means to ruthlessly weed out the poor prospects from your pipeline. Ask yourself this question about each opportunity on your list: "Why am I going to win this deal?" If you can't identify two unambiguously rock-solid differentiators that have quantifiable value to the customer, then the customer doesn't belong in your pipeline.

Effective qualification is addition by subtraction. It's the antithesis of pipeline mania. You will add to your available selling time by subtracting the sales opportunities that aren't valid before you waste time on them.

Instead of worrying about building your pipeline, focus on making sure that every sales opportunity you are working is worth that investment of your time. Analyze how you spend your selling time. How much is spent at each stage of your selling process? If you are like most salespeople, you are spending a disproportionate amount of your time with customers in the early stages of their decision cycles. In large measure, this is due to indecisive and ineffective qualification. It's hard to relinquish a potential customer who has some measure of interest in your product or service. But what if you could change that ratio? What if you could more quickly disqualify those sales opportunities that you aren't going to win and spend more time in the true value-delivering stages of the selling process?

That is the multiplier effect of effective qualification. Spend less time on marginal prospects, and win more orders from well-qualified opportunities.

CHAPTER 30

The Bulletproof Qualification Process

I BELIEVE THAT every sale you lose is not, in fact, a qualified sales opportunity.

Why?

When you lose a deal, the customer is saying to you that your product or service was not an exact match or even the best fit for their requirements. Someone else's product was. Depending on how many competitors were in on the deal, you might not have even been in second place. In which case, you have to question why you were even competing for this business.

How well are you qualifying your new customer sales opportunities? On the deals you lost, did you first qualify the prospects by determining whether they were interested in a product that was sort of like yours? Or mostly like yours? Or did they need exactly what you have to offer?

Wait, wait. I can hear you say, "What about the competition? What if they have a product just like mine? The customer was going to choose one of us. We just happened to lose this deal."

Well, let me ask you a question: Is there not at least one point of significant differentiation between your product or service and the competition's? Are your value propositions identical in every aspect? Even in competitive markets with highly commoditized products, there are differentiators. In which case, on lost deals, did you specifically qualify the customer on those unique aspects of your offering and value proposition?

When salespeople are prospecting for new leads, they tend to limit their search to customers who want to buy a product or service that is generally like theirs. But that approach can be a problem. It requires less work than searching and prospecting for customers whose requirements align exactly with what they have to sell. These two distinct approaches to business development and qualification yield two very different sets of sales opportunities. And results.

Salespeople are their own worst enemies in this regard. They have a fear of being too specific in their value proposition because they are afraid that it will limit the size of the pool of potential sales opportunities that they can develop.

However, as you learned in the previous chapter, your chances of success will increase if you do just the opposite. You don't want to broaden the field of prospects you have to comb through to find a qualified customer. You want to narrow it. You want to be relentless in your prospecting and qualification to find sales opportunities that are suited for precisely what you're selling. The outcome will be a much higher conversion rate, less competitive sales situations, and more stable pricing.

I want you to develop a bulletproof process for qualifying new sales opportunities. The stakes are high. Qualify correctly, and you'll wisely spend your selling time working with the right customers. Approach qualification casually, and you'll wonder why you are busy chasing down leads that turn out to be unqualified.

Bulletproofing qualification is a multistep process. This chapter covers the first step and the one major pitfall to avoid. In the next chapter, I'll cover qualifying on price and value.

Much like every topic that I have coached you on in this book—whether it is responsiveness or delivering value in your sales process—when you qualify sales opportunities, you have to focus on the specifics versus generalities. The more specific you are with the customer about your value, features, benefits, pricing, and support, the more likely you are to find a prospect who will be qualified to buy exactly what you are selling.

The first step of qualification is the most critical. Make a mistake at this stage, and you'll find yourself chasing after too many unqualified sales opportunities.

The first step of qualification offers two paths: category qualification and product qualification.

Category qualification is the default strategy for most salespeople. It means qualifying a customer who wants to buy a product or service that is similar to theirs. They are qualifying their leads as prospects not for their product per se but for the category of product or service they are selling.

Most companies provide their salespeople with what I call motherhood-and-apple-pie qualifying questions. They are designed to cast a broad net and snare as many potential sales opportunities as possible.

I had a client that sold test equipment. The company had four main competitors in its core market. One of the company's salespeople had a good nose for digging up sales opportunities that were being worked by his competitors. He thought that if one or more competitors were trying to capture a customer's business, then this must also be a prospect for him. So he would jump in with both feet, irrespective of whether the customer's needs were precisely aligned with his value proposition.

If you pursue a category qualification approach, it means you are more focused on a classic sales-is-a-numbers-game approach to selling. "Let's fill up the funnel and see how many pop out at the bottom." This has been the primary method for salespeople since the beginning of the twentieth century. It's a brute-force approach to sales that may yield some results but wastes both the seller's and prospect's time.

I worked with the CEO of a company that sold a somewhat commoditized product. A key differentiator was that the company possessed a unique capability to mass-customize the product it sold that the competition couldn't match. But it took extra sales work to find customers who could purchase the product in the requisite volume to justify the customization. Absent that, the company was just another face in the crowd, no better than any other seller in the market. The CEO's salespeople were trained to sell the customization service, but they never were comfortable with limiting themselves to prospecting for these specific prospects. They were more comfortable with broad category qualification—even though it was ultimately unproductive.

Category qualification is passive. That's why salespeople gravitate toward it. The bar is set pretty low, and it's easy to defend to your manager.

The alternative to category qualification is product qualification. A disciplined product qualification approach dictates that you are prospecting for customers that need exactly what you have to offer. They specifically need the unique value that your product and services provides and that differentiates you from your competitor.

To product-qualify a sales opportunity means to reach a preliminary agreement with the customer that the unique value you offer will be an essential criterion in the customer's decision making. This requires that you don't just run through your list of standard qualifying questions and check off enough boxes on a qualification checklist to show your boss that yours is a qualified sales opportunity.

I remember attending my first sales training class where I learned a reductive method of product qualification. We were trained to ask a series of A/B questions. The answer to each led to another A/B question in a long chain of questions designed to winnow down the available options and identify the features that the customer just couldn't live without. The increasingly specific A/B pairs were cleverly designed to have the customer choose between two options that we supported.

Product qualification requires that you simultaneously educate while you question. This is what should be happening during the discovery phase of your sales process. Discovery is not just about uncovering customers' requirements. It's also about winnowing down their requirements from the "wants" to the "must-haves" and educating them about how the must-haves correlate to the features and value provided by your product or service.

As a precursor to qualification, your primary sales task should be to identify sales opportunities whose key decision criteria precisely align with your unique value. This takes more work up front. It also requires the self-discipline to "catch and release" prospects who don't measure up to your qualification standards. If the closest you can get to a customer is category qualification, then you have to honestly assess how far off the mark are you. If another vendor has nailed product qualification with a prospect, then you need to determine whether this is an opportunity worth pursuing. It's always better to save your ammo (i.e., your selling time) for an opportunity to positively influence the outcome.

Take a moment to imagine what will happen to your sales results when your pipeline is composed primarily of prospects who are qualified to buy your specific product or service, as opposed to your category of product or service. Provided that you are a responsive and maximum value seller, the result will be compressed buying cycles, improved sales productivity, and more money in your pocket.

CHAPTER 31

Qualifying on Price and Value

THE SECOND STEP in your bulletproof qualification process is price qualification.

Salespeople are often too busy chasing a buck to really listen to the customer. They desperately cling to "sales opportunities" because they are loathe to kick any potential buyer to the curb. But, as a consequence, they skip what should be an essential early step in their sales process: qualifying the prospect on price. The purpose of qualifying your sales opportunities is to identify high-potential customers with requirements, if not appetites, for the exact product or service you are selling at the price for which you are offering it.

I once read an article in which the writer advised salespeople to avoid talking about price until they have "demonstrated the value" of their product or service. Unfortunately, there is a fundamental problem with that advice: You can't demonstrate the value of your product without talking about your price. And you shouldn't try. Value doesn't exist in the absence of pricing information.

Price qualification is simple and straightforward: You reach a preliminary agreement with the customer about the value that she will receive from your product in exchange for the price she is going to pay you. In other words, to qualify a sales opportunity on price, you have to reach a tentative agreement with the prospect that your price is proportional to her assessment of your product's value.

When you are talking to a prospect about the value of your product, what is the measure of that value? Value is not an abstract concept. It has to be quantifiable to have meaning for prospects.

Dictionary.com defines value as "the worth of something in terms of the amount of other things for which it can be exchanged." This means that you can express the value of your product or service, for example, in cost savings, improved productivity, or reduced customer churn, but for the full effect your customers must be able to measure the worth of that value in terms of the money they must pay to receive it. Customers have to be able to envision the return on that investment in terms that are meaningful to them.

You can tell your prospects, "Our customers have experienced an average of 19 percent growth in annual sales in the first three years of using our product." But the first thing they'd do is calculate what a 19 percent improvement in sales would be worth to them in terms of the investment they must make to realize that value. How can they make that necessary calculation if you are withholding pricing information? They can't.

Qualification on price and value doesn't mean that your prospects will be 100 percent in love with your price. But it does mean they agree that you're in the ballpark and that any further discussions about price will be a negotiation about deliverables, not a price objection.

As you have learned, your job as a salesperson is first and foremost to provide your customers with the information they need to make informed purchase decisions. The number one piece of information that your prospects want when they talk to you is pricing. After your prospects have spent time online researching your company and what it sells, they want to understand the value your products and services will provide them. This understanding cannot be reached without talking about price.

Price qualification's rightful place is early in the sales process, no later than during the discovery phase. Working with a sales opportunity beyond the discovery phase without qualifying it on price puts you on the fast track to a vicious sales cycle. In fact, price is a valid reason for you to disqualify a prospect. First, ask the right questions of prospects to fully understand their requirements and make sure these are aligned with your value proposition (aka product qualification.) Then clearly lay out the value, price, and the ROI they can expect from your solution, based on the prospect's stated requirements. If you can't reach a preliminary agreement on your value-for-price equation at this stage, then you probably need to walk away.

This begs the question: Can you get a price objection from a truly qualified prospect? The answer is no. You can't qualify a customer on price without disclosing your price. If you reach the preliminary qualifying agreement with the customer on the value-received-for-price-paid equation, then the customer is extremely unlikely to raise future objections to your pricing (barring an unexpected change in scope or circumstances).

A true price objection surfaced by your prospect at the end stages of the sales cycle usually means one of two things: (1) You misplaced your backbone at the moment of truth and didn't disqualify the prospect when you had the opportunity, or (2) you didn't fully disclose your price during qualification. If it is reason 1, then the prospect was never a true prospect for your product or service, and you wasted your valuable sales time on someone who was never going to buy from you. If the answer is reason 2, then you misled the prospect about your value proposition, and it will be difficult to rebuild your credibility and win the order.

Over the course of many years, I have successfully taught clients and salespeople four rules of thumb about price qualification:

1. *Be direct with the prospect about your pricing.* Salespeople have developed an unhealthy fear of the price question. They want to stuff it away in a closet and forget about it. They fear that any discussion of price will frighten off the customer. But that is exactly the point. There is no mystery to qualifying on price. Do what you do best. Ask the right questions to fully understand the customer's requirements and make sure there's alignment with your value, features, and specs. And then talk price and value based on the customer's requirements.

2. *Price qualification means that you reach a preliminary agreement that your price is proportional to the customer's assessment of your product's or service's value.* Qualification on price and value doesn't mean that you'll never have another discussion about price with the customer. But it does mean that conversation will more likely be centered on scope and deliverables as the means to adjust the pricing to align with the customer's requirements.

3. *A price objection is a valid reason to disqualify a prospect.* Disqualification on price must take place early in your sales process. A true price objection from a prospect late in the sales cycle means that you weren't transparent in providing your pricing and didn't disqualify the prospect when you had the opportunity. Consequently, the customer was never a true sales opportunity, and you wasted your selling time on someone who was never going to buy from you.

4. *Beware of the price-qualified customer who keeps pushing back on price.* If you do a good job of qualifying the prospect on price, but he keeps pushing back on price while ostensibly still moving forward with his buying process, then you should proceed with caution. It's possible the buyer has a hidden agenda and is using you in order to advance it. In one very large deal early in my career, the price-qualified prospect kept raising price objections. Unfortunately, I made the mistake of responding to these objections because I didn't have the experience to understand that the prospect was using me as a leverage point to negotiate a better deal with the competition. It was a painful lesson learned.

Product qualification and price qualification are simple and practical tools that will help you maintain your focus on those sales opportunities that have a higher probability of providing a great return on your investment of selling time.

CHAPTER 32

Objections and Qualification

WHY ARE YOU so afraid of an objection?

Objections are not potential sales roadblocks. They are opportunities.

That's right. Objections are opportunities to develop a more complete understanding of your prospects' requirements and to engage with them on a deeper level. They are also opportunities to protect yourself from selling to prospects who will never buy from you. In either case, they represent an opportunity for you to make a sound decision about how to invest your selling time.

In the traditional literature of selling, objections are to be "overcome," "managed," or "handled." The assumption is that an objection is dangerous to your chances of winning a deal. So the customers' expectations must be managed in order to overcome the damage that the objection could cause. And customers have to be handled in order to shift their attention away from their perception of your deficits and toward your strengths.

I am always amused at the notion of overcoming objections—as if brute force and ignoring the customer's concerns would make them evaporate. In one of the sales training classes that my first employer sent me to, we were taught to handle objections by essentially ignoring them. The technique we were drilled to use was the just-suppose method. Let's assume I was selling a meal delivery service that companies used to deliver breakfast and lunch to employees between the hours of 8 A.M. and 2 P.M.

I developed a lead with a company that needed meals delivered to its employees. But once I had a meeting with the decision maker, I learned that they had a requirement only for dinners to be delivered (to engineers who worked late). The just-suppose method was supposed to handle that objection by saying, "Well, Mr. Prospect, just suppose that we could deliver dinner, would you be interested in buying from us?" If the answer was yes, then I was supposed to sell him on the virtues of breakfast and lunch delivery, even though his company didn't need it.

Unfortunately, ignorance is still how many salespeople deal with objections. Problem is, that ignores the positive sales opportunities that objections present.

Answer this question: What is an objection? (No peeking ahead!)

An objection is simply a question. If buying is about getting the information required to make a sound decision quickly, then objections are questions that need an answer to help the customer move forward with you in the buying process. If you attempt to overlook, overcome, or manage your customers' objections, their buying processes will screech to a halt. They won't move to the next step until you've provided the missing information.

Imagine that a customer has a concern about a particular aspect of your offering. ("It looks like it will require too many internal resources to support your product.") Or he has an incomplete understanding about how a particular feature operates. ("I don't think we'll see the improvements in throughput you projected in your proposal.") Or maybe he just doesn't understand the payback his company will receive from its investment. ("Our IRR on this project is too low.")

Customers raise objections because they need more information or greater clarity about a particular topic. As a salesperson, it may be natural for you to assume a defensive posture when hit with an objection—to try to explain away customers' concerns and to justify your current proposal or approach. These are the last things you want to do at that point in time.

Instead of playing defense, your job is to convert the customer's objection into a question and to respond to it so that the customer can start moving forward again toward a decision.

For example, let's take the three preceding customer objections and turn them into questions that address their concerns.

- "It looks like it will require too many internal resources to support your product." The question this objection asks is, "Typically, how many people, and with which particular skills sets, are required to install and support the operation of your product?"

- "I don't think we'll see the improvements in throughput you projected in your proposal." The question you need to answer is, "How will your system integrate with our current processes, and do you have any examples of how your other customers have accomplished this?"

- "Our IRR on this project is too low." You would convert that into this question: "Can you take me through the assumptions and calculations you used to project the return we'll earn on our investment in your technology?"

- Then answer each of these questions for the customer.

Keep in mind that an objection represents a go/no-go moment in a sales process. You have a decision to make regarding the objection. Can you answer the question? Does your answer illuminate the value and solution that you are providing? Most important, does your answer directly address the customer's concerns enough to comfortably start moving forward with you again? If not, perhaps the objection should be your exit plan.

I coach salespeople to survey the customer after answering an objection. Simply ask for an assessment of how well you answered the objection. "Does that answer your question?" "Did we fully address your concerns?" "On a scale of one to five, with one being the highest, how did we do?" Then ask where you stand. "Mr. Prospect, on this particular issue, how would you rank our solution compared to the alternatives you are considering?"

Think again of the New Sales Funnel (see Figure 11–2). As customers move down through the funnel, they not only have fewer questions, but they also should have fewer objections.

As such, look at each customer objection as an opportunity to requalify that sales opportunity. Qualification is not a one-time event. As described in Chapter 10, the mere act of moving through a buying process will necessarily change your customers. They learn new information about how to solve their requirements, and consequently it's not unusual to see their priorities shift in fairly significant ways. Therefore, the product and price qualification you previously performed may no longer be valid.

If in the latter stages of the buying process, a customer raises a significant objection to your offer, it may be a clear sign that you are fighting for second place. There appears to be an unwritten rule in selling that once you have embarked on a deal, you must see it through until the bitter end—even if you believe with some certainty that you are not going to win. Remember, you have to manage your inventory of selling time very carefully, and lost causes don't help you make quota.

Think back to Chapter 9. Have you "won the sale"? Substantial objections in the latter stages of a sales cycle usually indicate no.

Finally, I want to talk about customer truthfulness and objections.

According to one school of thought, certain objections are really smoke screens, and customers who voice them are being less than truthful. Take, for instance, the objection that really isn't an objection: "We're not interested."

"We're not interested" isn't an objection because customers aren't objecting to anything other than your presence and the fact that you're consuming their valuable time in an attempt to make them interested in your product.

Too many sales trainers would have you believe that customers are interested but being coy and playing hard to get. According to these people, what customers really want is for you to press your case harder, be more aggressive, and make them want to love you. Although there is an element of courtship in any customer relationship, it's a bit absurd to presume that customers play hard to get in order to increase your ardor for selling to them.

So what does it mean when prospects tell you, "We're not interested?" Usually, it means they are not interested. It isn't an objection. It's a fact.

Believe it or not, sometimes a prospect just isn't interested in what you're selling, even if you believe that your product or service is a perfect fit.

What motivation would a customer have to lie to a salesperson about a lack of interest? And if the customer tells a lie to get rid of you, how could you justify spending any more of your limited selling time trying to convince a liar to do business with you?

I own my own company. Salespeople who think I need their products approach me every day. When I tell one that I am not interested, what I really mean is that I'm not interested.

CHAPTER 33

Building a Productive Pipeline

"WELL, THE BUYERS were just liars."

I was riding the Amtrak Acela up to Boston when a cell phone–toting salesperson sitting behind me uttered this immortal couplet. It was the last day of the sales month, and my fellow passenger, whom I will call Jon, clearly was attempting to rationalize his failure to close a much-needed piece of business to one of his bosses.

Jon's unintentional verse was almost Shakespearean in the tale of drama, treachery, and tragedy it told in just six short words. It combined a scathing indictment of the fecklessness of the prospective customer with a transparent attempt to shed any responsibility for his obvious failure to win an order that he had no doubt forecast with a high degree of certainty in an attempt to (a) curry favor and ingratiate himself with his bosses or (b) keep his job.

How often have you been caught in this trap of overcommitting on a forecast for a particular sales opportunity even though you hadn't truly qualified the customer for your specific product and price? And then you were forced to stand in front of the entire sales team to defend the indefensible.

Without effectively qualifying customers, you have no solid understanding of the criteria they will use to make their purchase decision. In these situations, I have found that the vociferousness with which salespeople defend their actions or refuse to take responsibility for them, just like

Jon, is usually in inverse proportion to the level of qualification that took place. You don't want to be that guy.

Strengthening your pipeline is an important task. It requires that you be utterly pragmatic and a bit ruthless in how you assess the quality of the sales opportunities on which you are working. The goal is to hack away the deadwood that populates your pipeline and consumes valuable selling time that you need to devote to customers who actually will make the decision to purchase from you.

A pipeline can only be as strong as its weakest link. Invariably that weakest link is the salesperson. Is your pipeline populated by sales opportunities that are past their expiration dates? Which prospects are not truly product- and price-qualified? Which ones are you clinging to in an attempt to lull yourself into believing that there is safety in numbers?

All these behaviors can lead to a vicious sales cycle. A salesperson loads up a pipeline with weak, unqualified sales opportunities in an effort to demonstrate hard work to the manager. These weak prospects consume a disproportionate amount of the salesperson's selling time, leaving little time to devote to strong prospects. Which leads to difficult conversations like the one Jon was having with his boss.

I only heard the last line of the conversation between Jon and his boss, who I'll call Tracy. But I can easily imagine what transpired before I tuned in.

"Hey, Tracy. This is Jon."

"Jon." Silence.

"How's it going?"

Silence. Tracy was not going to make this easy for Jon.

"Uh, so we just finished the meeting with Consolidated."

Silence. Tracy liked torturing salespeople with his silence.

"Well, uh, it didn't go as we hoped."

"Why not?"

"They decided to go with the other guys."

"Why?"

"I dunno. It seems like they changed their decision criteria."

"Why?"

"I dunno. Probably the other guys can do something we can't."

"And we're just finding this out now?"

"Well, they didn't say anything before."

"Didn't say? Or you didn't ask?"

"Uh, well, I don't know."

"Actually, Jon, it sounds like they made their decision a while ago."

"No, not at all."

"Wasn't it just last week that you were absolutely positive that you were going to close the Consolidated order this month?"

"Well, the buyers were just liars."

Here are three strategies to strengthen your pipeline and pave the way for easier forecast meetings with your sales manager.

1. Disqualify the losers. Let's be blunt. Too many sales opportunities in your pipeline are losers. I am not using "loser" as a pejorative to insult these customers. What I mean is that these deals are losers for you. That your chances of winning them are extremely low. But by virtue of the fact that they are in your pipeline means that you are spending selling time you can't afford to waste on sales opportunities that will never turn into an order for you.

Working with the losers will have a measurable negative impact on your sales. Let's begin by looking at your selling time. Various studies show that salespeople spend the majority of their work week on nonselling activities. An Accenture/CSO Insights study found that, on average, sales reps spent only 42 percent of their time selling. Indeed, one study found that high-performing sales reps spend only 55 percent of their time selling. So in order to make the math easy, let's assume that you spend only 50 percent, or two and a half days, of your work week selling. How much time do you spend on the losers? You may say that you don't spend that much time with them. But if they are losers, they shouldn't get a minute of your sales time.

If you're at 90 percent of quota but you can increase the amount of selling time you have by 10 percent by disqualifying all the losers in your pipeline, you suddenly have a chance to use the strategies from this part of the book to successfully qualify sales opportunities that can put you over the top.

How do you know that you have successfully weeded the losers out of your pipeline? Here's the clue. Stop being defensive when discussing certain sales opportunities in a sales meeting or in a pipeline review with your manager. And start having positive proactive discussions about sales strategies and closing deals.

2. Requalify the qualified. Things change. Recall my Uncertainty Principle of Selling from Chapter 10. The very act of buying necessarily changes the buyer's requirements. As buyers learn more about the potential solutions for their requirements, they will also learn more about their requirements. As they gather more information and, most important, insights from various sellers about how to meet their needs and address their pain points, they become more educated about the existing options. They become smarter. One outcome of this change is the very real possibility that they are no longer your qualified prospects. Perhaps their needs have grown beyond your capabilities. Or they have discovered that they can resolve their pain points with a significantly smaller investment than they originally planned. You have to stay on top of this at all times. If you're struggling to meet quota, can you really afford to spend time working a prospect that is no longer qualified?

Here's another reason to requalify sales opportunities: You can't take your prospects' interest for granted. Their interest in you and your solution is like an organic entity—they are subject to change. Just because they were once qualified does not mean that they still are.

Lastly, you also can't count on the customer to tell you that you are no longer in the game. Customers will go radio silent and just stop communicating with you when they're no longer considering your offer. This can be frustrating. However, they also have no incentive to tell you bad news. No one likes delivering bad news. Besides, perhaps the decision maker needs to tell her superiors that she evaluated multiple vendors before making a choice, so you are kept in the dark about the company's intentions even though you are no longer under consideration. You're still selling, but the customer is no longer buying!

3. Plan for the end game. What is the game plan for all the sales opportunities in your pipeline? How will you get them from where they are today to an order? It's important to know this for every customer in the pipeline.

Selling is a team effort. For a team to succeed, every player has to understand his or her role. Keep in mind that one of the most essential members of your sales team is your customer. Selling is not something that happens to customers. They fully participate in the process (though they like to call it buying). Like any individual player, your customers have to be fully informed about the role they are playing and the expectations you have for their performance in order for the team to achieve its goals.

Invariably this plan will change as the result of your sales efforts. But you still need to map it out. It's an integral part of answering the question, "Why is this customer going to buy from you?" It's not all about the product or your price. As I have stressed throughout this book, any success you experience will be due as much to how you sell as to what you sell. How are you going to get your customers across the finish line? The answer is by bringing them into your plan, committed to playing their role to the end.

In sum, strengthening your pipeline means nothing more than effectively qualifying—and continually requalifying—your customers as they move through their buying processes. This means that you have to revisit hard questions about your value and suitability for their needs, their budgets, and their time frames.

PART VII

Mastering Stories
That Sell

CHAPTER 34

Becoming an Effective Content Curator and Provider

IN THIS INTERNET age, we have seen the rise of the so-called empowered (or enabled or educated) customer. Given ready access to a trove of information online, it would be easy to make the mistake of believing that the importance of a salesperson's role as a provider of information to the customer had diminished. In fact, the opposite is true. More than ever, salespeople have a critical role to play in helping customers gather the information they need to make fast and low-cost purchase decisions.

Undoubtedly, the role a salesperson plays in the dissemination of information to customers has changed. No longer are they the sole distributors of content about the products and services they sell. Now a company's website and various social media channels are the key distribution points of the pool of content it has produced about the products and services it markets. The company makes strategic and tactical decisions about how to communicate that content to potential customers, whether by blog, tweet, e-mail, brochure, slide deck, webinar, data sheet, phone call, or other means.

When asked to define "content," salespeople tend to have a parochial point of view. They believe that content consists of information that their companies developed to supply to their customers.

Unfortunately, that narrow perspective creates a mismatch with the information needs of their prospects. The problem for salespersons is that their customers have a much broader definition of, and requirement for, content. To customers, content is the sum total of the information and insights they need to gather in order to make a fully informed purchase decision in the least time possible.

Marketers have become so prolific in creating content about their offerings that it has created another problem for buyers. Tony O'Driscoll from the Fuqua School of Business at Duke University wrote an article in 2013 in which he described how the wealth of content being created and consumed had left buyers asking, "So what? I have all this content. But what does it mean for me? And how can I use it to make better purchase decisions?" Customers have access to a wealth of content. What are they missing? Context.

In their buying cycles, customers are looking to get not only the specifics about particular products and services but also third-party information, insights borne from industry-specific expertise and experience, and research data points that will help illuminate the overall context for the decisions they have to make. For instance, an informed buyer may need to know where the technology is evolving in your product segment, not only for you but also for your competition. She may need to know what her own competitors have done or are doing with products and technology similar to yours. She may need to have an understanding of what technologies will be coming to market in the near future that could impact her company's position if adopted by a competitor first. This customer is looking to the salesperson to be the conduit for all of her unmet information requirements. The salesperson has to think more universally about the information he needs to supply to help this customer make a decision. In this sense, the salesperson has to be both an effective content provider and an insightful content curator—a trusted source of pertinent information and relevant insights that he personally selected to support the buyer's decision making.

Research supports the importance of the salesperson as content provider. One study found that salespeople who are effective and responsive content providers dramatically increased their chances of sales success. In a 2010 study by DemandGen and Genius.com titled "Inside the Mind of the B2B Buyer," 95 percent of B2B customers surveyed said that the seller they chose "provided them with ample content to help them navigate through each stage of the buying process." On the surface, this may seem self-evident, but let's dig a little deeper. Remember, first and foremost, that your prospects won't move from one step of their buying process to the next until their information requirements for the current stage are met. Do a great job in curating and providing information that moves the customer to act, and you'll be rewarded with orders. How often can your sales actions have such a direct and definitive impact on your sales success?

In the same 2010 study, 80 percent of respondents indicated that "timeliness of providing content" was a key selection criterion in their choice of vendor. In other words, being a responsive seller who provides needed content quickly helps win orders. What's more, 62 percent of respondents in a survey of B2B buyers said that the "consistent and relevant communications" provided by the seller was key in influencing their decision making about a solution and the solution provider.

Dr. O'Driscoll described how the Internet overloads people with content without providing context. The same holds true for your customers. Buyers are looking to the salesperson to provide some clarity and a way to make sense of the mountains of content they have uncovered. Sellers who can create value for their customers by consistently serving them information that helps them develop a more informed perspective on their upcoming decisions dramatically increase their odds of winning the business.

Lastly, it is essential that you, the salesperson, think like your buyers in order to identify relevant and valuable sources of contextual information. One study found that customers are searching a wider range of information sources to support their decision making:

- 48 percent used a wider variety of sources of information (beyond vendor websites).

- 59 percent engaged with peers.

- 48 percent followed industry conversations online.

- 37 percent posted questions on social media looking for advice.

Salespeople have to engage with this same range of information sources on the buyer's behalf. If you can do this for your customers, the research shows that you will increase your opportunities to win their business.

Here are three simple steps to becoming a more effective content curator and provider:

1. *Create an information road map for each sales opportunity.* As the salesperson, you need to thoroughly map out the entire set of in-house and curated content that each customer will need to make an informed purchase decision and the decision to purchase your product. As discussed in the previous chapter, as soon as a qualified sales opportunity enters your pipeline, you should have a plan for moving with the customer through the remainder of the buying process. Unless you're new to your company, you should have the experience and product knowledge to complete this information road map on your own. If not, have a mentor guide you through this process the first time.

The purpose of the road map is to be prepared to answer your customer's questions in the shortest time possible. You've been down the road before with previous deals that you have closed. Use that experience to develop a library of the content that you will need at each step of the customer's buying process. You'll then be prepared to anticipate the customer's questions and be absolutely responsive to them.

2. *Identify relevant third-party sources of information.* On a deal-by-deal basis, define a list of third-party sources from which you can select relevant content that will deliver value to the customer. If you concentrate your sales efforts on a particular industry or vertical market, then you should already be aware of what these are. If not, do some online research, or ask your customers about the sources of information they use.

Your goal is to make customers smarter, in a global sense, about their problem, their requirements, and the value of the solution that you can provide. Yes, customers can go online and find this information for themselves. But they will be content to outsource this to you—if you can deliver. Envision the credibility and trust you will build with your customers if you do.

3. *Aggressively use available tools to find valuable content.* It will be up to you to go online and find the information your customers need. Be consistent in your use of available easy-to-use tools to simplify this task. Here are a few quick ideas about finding relevant content that would be valued by your prospect:

- *Set up Google Alerts for every qualified prospect.* Track multiple key-words associated with your prospect's company, the primary indus-try it serves, and its key competitors. Set up an alert for your products/services with the customer's industry. Check these daily for content that will provide value to the prospect. Don't hesitate to send e-mails with links to relevant information you uncovered. "Dear Ms. Prospect: I think you'll be interested in this article I ran across this morning about the ROI companies in your industry can expect to receive from investments in technology like that we have proposed to you." Do this consistently, and the customer will come to depend on the value that you provide in your communications.

- *Subscribe to key blogs in the customer's market space.* Provide links to customers to postings from bloggers in their industry that dis-cuss the problems solved and benefits received from solutions like yours. These articles can provide the customer with insights about pain points and possible solutions from the perspective of industry peers. Make certain that you read everything that you send to the customer. It will make you smarter about your customers and develop your own expertise in their industries.

- *Find third-party analyst or academic research on your product cate-gory.* Even if all you can find online is the abstract from a research report, you can usually learn enough information from that to understand its conclusions. Provide these to your customer—even if the data doesn't 100 percent support your position. This is a great way to develop trust and credibility by showing that you are not trying to hide any data that would be useful for the customer to know. (You always have to assume that the customer will find this data independently or that your competition will provide it.) If you were working on a big enough deal, it may even be worth buying the report for the customer.

- *Search YouTube for videos that address issues such as installation or implementation or that feature concerns the prospect may have for a solution like yours.* The more you can find, the more it will help to demonstrate the widespread acceptance of the product you sell.

- *Check resources such as SlideShare for presentations that are relevant to the customer's upcoming decision.* SlideShare is an incredible source of relevant presentations, industry data, and research studies.

- *Search online for industry conferences, and look for presentations that are relevant to the prospect's buying cycle.* Find a link to the conference proceedings. Or e-mail the presenters and ask for a copy of the slides. This practice will again demonstrate your engagement in the customer's buying process and your determination to help the customer make the most informed decision possible.

Being an effective content curator and provider requires an investment of time and thought on the part of the salesperson. But this investment is usually the difference between a successful salesperson and one who is always playing catch-up on quota.

CHAPTER 35

Four Questions to Build Compelling Sales Stories

WELL-CRAFTED AND polished sales stories are the most effective method for quickly and powerfully conveying to a prospect why an existing customer decided to purchase your product and got value from its use. Well-told stories create an indelible impact on a customer. Stories are an essential sales tool to differentiate you and your offering in the mind of your customer.

Since the dawn of humankind, stories have been used to provide information and insights. Before written alphabets existed, stories were used to communicate the traditions of a society from one generation to another. Some philosophers believe that stories, such as cultural mythologies, have become embedded in our DNA through thousands of years and countless generations of retelling. Just look at our popular culture to see that our most popular modes of entertainment are forms of storytelling. TV shows, movies, books, music, and even video games are all about telling a story. Stories are popular because of their power to sweep up listeners or viewers into worlds other than their own.

Perhaps this is why Plato proposed banning storytellers in ancient Greece more than 2,500 years ago. In the rational society that Plato envisioned, stories didn't appeal to the logical or rational side of listeners but to their feelings and emotions. Emotions are not rational, so Plato wanted stories banned. But it is the emotions and feelings that will make your sales stories so powerful.

Unfortunately, for most salespeople, the "story" they have to tell is a rather boring recitation that stars the features and benefits of their products and services, instead of a crisp, concise tale that conveys the tangible value a customer received.

Let's set aside business for a minute. If I were to ask you, "What's your story?" how would you answer? If you were like most people, you would recite a history of your life. "I'm 45 years old. I was born and raised in Bozeman, Montana. I have two sisters and a brother. I went to college in Wisconsin and studied electrical engineering. I work as a sales account executive for a chip manufacturer. I'm married and have two sons." A factual recitation of your life's milestones is not a story. If that were a script for a TV show, it would be about as riveting as the phone book.

How about this story instead? "My wife and I are lifelong baseball fans. We play in a softball league, and between us we coach and manage our two sons' Little League teams. Our dream is to attend a baseball game in each of the major league ballparks. Every summer since the boys were in school, we pack up our SUV and spend two weeks on a driving and camping trip to a different ballpark. This year it's Southern California. Angel Stadium. Dodger Stadium. I can smell the grilled Dodger Dogs now. And at Petco Park in San Diego? Fish tacos!"

How can you divorce yourself from an overreliance on facts and features and put the power of the story into your selling?

Let's start with an overview of some basic ground rules about effective sales stories.

- *Keep it simple and short.* The key to a great story is to keep it simple and short. If you try to accomplish too much with a story, or if you make it too complex or too long, then the prospect won't be able to understand it, let alone remember it. And neither will you.

- *Use simple detail to draw the prospect into the picture.* Stories become memorable when they draw your buyer into them. (Why does a TV series attract and retain your interest? Because part of you identifies with the challenges faced by the story's protagonist.) Your stories must relate to your prospects' most common challenges and pain points. To help your customers identify with the subjects of your stories, it's helpful to employ a little detail. Always give the characters in your stories a first name. Use their company's name (or a pseudonym if they object to your using their real name).

- *Illustrate a defining moment of value.* Sales stories should communicate your value proposition by illustrating the defining moments that existing customers experience with your product or service. You have to show the insight that the subjects of your story gained about their business or the problem they were attempting to solve by using your product or service. As a prospect listens to your story of how customers like them worked with you to solve a problem like theirs, they will picture in their mind what it would be like if they used your product or service. It's like taking a mental test drive of what you're offering. This mental test drive, in which customers envision themselves using your product, is a distinct and important step in their buying processes.

- *Use a story to provide insight and context.* Salespeople can fill prospects to the brim with raw facts and figures about the features and benefits of their products and services. It's what they do best. But your customers are searching for some context to digest and make sense of the content they have consumed. A concise story about why a current customer made the decision to purchase your solution and how that customer is using it to solve problems and eliminate pain points is one of the most effective sources of context for a new prospect to use in decision making.

Before we build some sales stories, allow me to answer the questions that every salesperson has about them.

Where do the stories come from? Sales stories come from you and your experiences or from your colleagues and their experiences. These stories should be freely shared among all salespeople on your team. They are company assets. Once you have created a story, write it down and share it with your peers.

In an ideal world marketing and sales would collaborate to create customer stories with the broadest relevance to your current sales opportunities. But last I checked, many of us don't live in that world. So you, the salesperson, need to take responsibility for creating these stories. As you'll soon see, it's easy to do.

How long should my stories be? Each of your sales stories should take no more than one minute to present. Shorter is better, so 30 to 45 seconds would have more impact. Let me put that in context for you. The average American native English speaker will speak about 150 words per minute (and usually less). This means that your effective sales story will be less than half a page long. In fact, this paragraph and the next, combined, are only about 150 words long.

There are two reasons for this time limit. First, if the stories are any longer, they will become too complex and difficult for you to remember. Which means that you won't use them. Second, if your story drags on for longer than one minute, your prospect will stop hearing your words and start hearing, "blah-blah-blah." "Blah" is not how you want the prospect to remember you, your product, or your company.

How many stories do I need? You need a core of at least three stories. This is enough to cover a wide array of potential customers. If you need more, ask your colleagues to share some of theirs with you. Play nice and reciprocate.

Now let's begin crafting your compelling sales stories.

The first step is to identify a current customer whose story will have broad appeal to potential buyers.

The second step involves answering four simple questions:

1. *What problem was your customer trying to solve?* What was the primary pain point the customer had to resolve? You have to be specific and to the point. You can't be overly broad in your description of the problem because that will make it difficult for

your prospect to identify with what the current customer was experiencing before purchasing your product.

2. *Why was your expertise relevant to your customer?* Why did the customer reach out to you or your company to solve the problem? What reason were you given? Did the customer go on your website and research your company and product before engaging with you? What did the customer learn about your company that led to a talk with you? For instance, maybe the customer wanted to expand into Latin America and downloaded a case study from your website that detailed your experience setting up operations for another client in Brazil.

3. *Why did the customer buy from you?* What were the specific decision criteria the customer used to select your product? Why were you chosen over all the competitors? Or why did the customer choose to buy a new system from you instead of staying with an existing system? Be specific about the customer's rationale for selecting you. If you don't know for certain, call and ask.

4. *What value has the customer received from your product/service?* This should be easy to answer. What tangible and quantifiable value has the customer received from your product or service? This is the capper to the story. You can't finish a story with an everyone-lived-happily-ever-after fairytale ending. It needs to be specific. Buyers remember numbers and forget generalities.

Once you've gathered the information from answering the four questions, write down your story. This gives you a script from which to practice. (I'll talk about presenting your stories in the next chapter.) Here's a sample:

Larry is VP of Ops at a large multinational widget manufacturer. He said to me, "Andy, we have a problem increasing throughput on our main production line, and we're missing our forecast by 10 percent every month." He read an article in *Forbes* about our process control software and our experience working with similarly sized manufacturers to maximize their output. Ultimately, Larry bought from us because we were able to demonstrate to him how our system would decrease downtime and increase his manufacturing yield by 30 percent over the first 12 months. In fact, he hit that target in eight months and earned a 15 percent rate of return on his investment in our system in the first year alone.

That's 120 words. 45 seconds. Boom!

Remember: Simple, well-crafted stories will be more memorable than any facts or figures you can provide to your prospects.

CHAPTER 36

Are Your Stories Worth Repeating?

YOUR SALES stories have to be memorable and worth repeating. This means that they have to be easy for someone to retell. How do you make that happen?

Let's start with the story itself. You have to remember that the exclusive audience for your story is not the person to whom you initially tell it, even if that person is the final decision maker. Every sales story you tell has multiple audiences.

It is always possible that your customer is an autocratic organization with only one decision maker who doesn't solicit input or advice before making a purchase. But it is far more likely that your customers are normal companies with multiple people and departments involved in identifying potential solutions, qualifying vendors, making recommendations, and reaching decisions. Some companies may have multiple layers of approval that need to occur before the final decision is made at the C-level. Whatever the situation, you want to make sure that everyone who participates in the decision-making process hears your stories.

You may only have one opportunity to tell a story, but that doesn't mean that other people inside your customer's organization don't need to hear it. Your objective is to have your stories retold throughout your customer's company.

The person most likely to initiate the telling and retelling of your stories throughout your customer's organization will be your internal sales advocate(s). This is your sponsor—the person who believes that you have the solution that best meets the organization's requirements and will work on your behalf to help colleagues arrive at the same conclusion. Most likely it was one of your sales stories that helped win the sale with this individual and convince him to act as your internal salesperson.

For your internal advocates to successfully work on your behalf, you have to give them the tools that make their job easy. Working internally they will have exactly the same challenge that you have when you sell. Their colleagues are busy with their own responsibilities, and they will likely not have the time to invest in becoming as familiar with all of the details of your product's features and benefits as your advocate. And even if they did, dry facts and figures are not very interesting or memorable in the context of a competitive sales situation.

Your advocates have to be able to simply and easily communicate the value of your product, service, and company to multiple audiences throughout their organizations. The best and most effective advocacy tool you can provide them are your sales stories. What you hope is that these new audiences will in turn be moved to retell your stories to other internal audiences.

The more memorable your story, the more often it will be retold. When this happens, your value, features, benefits, and reputation invariably are amplified and solidified. This is the so-called telephone effect kicking in and working to your advantage.

What's the telephone effect? When you were a young kid, do you remember playing the game called Telephone?

The rules were pretty simple. You and your friends sat on the floor in a big circle. One person started the game by whispering a short piece of gossip or fiction, usually something slanderous about one of the kids in the circle, into the ear of the kid sitting to his left. That kid in turn whispered what she had heard into the ear of the kid sitting to her left. And on and around the story traveled from ear to ear until the last kid to have heard the telephone message stood up and repeated what he thought he'd heard. What started out as, say, "Jack and Jill went up the hill to fetch a pail of water" invariably turns into "Jill hijacked a pill truck with Gayle, her daughter."

This same dynamic is in play with the stories and the presentations you tell your prospects. You need to harness the power of the telephone dynamic to your sales advantage. The value of your solution and the value it provided to the customer who was the subject of the story will be amplified as it is retold. This is not necessarily a bad thing in terms of winning the business. (In Chapter 39, I'll show you how to manage customer expectations after you win the order.)

Think about the advantage that your internal advocate will enjoy compared to that of a competitor who doesn't have sales stories to tell. Competitors' advocates are left to show data sheets to colleagues. It takes the advocate longer to communicate the value of your competitor's solutions, and the decision cycle for that product begins to lengthen and slow down.

However, armed with compelling stories, your value and credibility grow as your stories pass through multiple hands. With each retelling, one more person takes the mental test drive and envisions the value and benefits of using your product. A story compresses the amount of time required to communicate and understand your value proposition, shortening the decision cycle. That is the power of story.

So what can you do to increase the memorability of your stories?

Follow the four-question structure from the previous chapter. The key to repeatable stories is to make certain they follow a common structure that quickly answers the four simple questions in logical order. These questions should become your mantra. (In fact, it will become the common form you use during the discovery phase of your sales cycle to understand why your prospect made the decision to purchase the product or service that you are going to replace.)

- What problems were they trying to solve?

- Why was your expertise relevant to the problem they were trying to solve?

- Why did they select your company and product/service?

- What value did the customer receive from your product/service?

Use memorable detail to draw in the prospect. To make your stories more relatable and memorable, use characters with a name and include dialog. Don't start a story by saying, "We have this customer who has used our product for two years and our main point of contact there is a big supporter of the system." Instead say, "Kevin is VP of Finance at KJ Technologies and has been a customer for two years. When we first met, he said to me, 'Andy, I've got a problem, and I saw that you helped my competitor.'" Details like these draw in listeners and get them to visualize themselves in the story. The dialog humanizes the story and makes it more real. It is no longer just you telling a random story. Kevin's story resonates with your buyer, who is dealing with the same problem now.

If your current customer doesn't want the company name used in the story, just omit it. Using the first name and title of your point of contact will be sufficient.

Practice, practice, practice. As the old joke goes, the only way to get to Carnegie Hall is to "Practice, man, practice!"

The same applies to your sales stories. How are you going to get to an order with your stories? Practice. Practice. Practice. You have to memorize and rehearse your stories so thoroughly that their telling becomes second nature to you.

To facilitate the memorization of your stories, as discussed in the previous chapter, write down all of your sales stories just as you would tell them, using complete sentences.

Then memorize them word for word. Don't sort of memorize them or treat them as bullet points to guide you. Telling a story is not the moment for improvisation. This is one of the most powerful tools you have to communicate your value to a customer. Don't wing it. Be prepared.

Once they are memorized, rehearse your stories in front of your colleagues. Every week in your sales meeting, set aside a few minutes to stand up in front of your peers and rehearse your presentation. Have someone record you on a smartphone so you can study your telling of the story and improve your presentation.

Why is it so important to memorize and rehearse your stories?

First, you have to keep them short to increase their impact. If you have a story that is 120 words long and takes 45 seconds to tell, it will always be that length if you memorize and retell it word for word. However, if you just treat the script as a guideline you will turn a 45-second story into a five-minute epic as you add extraneous and unnecessary filler during the telling.

Second, you have to keep stories short so that they can be remembered and retold. This is one of their primary powers. You have to make it easy for your internal advocate. If necessary, give your advocate some assistance. One salesperson I've coached sends the 150-word script for her sales stories to her advocates so that they can actually memorize them.

The power of stories to communicate insights and value is undeniable. If they are used correctly, sales stories are a powerful tool that can be retold to help spread your sales message and help you close orders.

CHAPTER 37

Integrating Stories into Your Selling Process

SALES STORIES can be used with great impact at any number of points in your selling process. Of course, the prerequisite is that you have the sales stories developed, edited, memorized, thoroughly rehearsed, and ready to use. (I can't stress enough the need to rehearse your stories. Salespeople like to believe that they can talk their way through any situation. Let me assure you, that is not the case.)

Here are some strategies about using sales stories during various stages of your sales cycle:

Prospecting. Let's say you're prospecting, making cold calls on the phone, and you manage to get through to the name on your list. The first question that customer will ask is, "What do you do?" How are you going to answer?

Like most salespeople, you have probably been trained to develop and present your elevator pitch as an icebreaker. Invariably elevator pitches are focused on you and what you do. "We've been in business 29 years …" "We help companies achieve …" "We transform our customers' …" "We work with customers to increase …"

The problem here is that you are answering the wrong question. The wording may have been, "What do you do?" But what the customer was really asking was, "What can you do for me?"

John Steinbeck was one of America's greatest storytellers. In his epic novel of California, *East of Eden*, he wrote, "If a story is not about the hearer he [or she] will not listen . . . The strange and foreign is not interesting—only the deeply personal and familiar." This is why the sell-centric elevator pitch more often than not falls on deaf ears. It isn't about the customer. It's about you.

That's why sales stories are so powerful. In the same length of time as your elevator pitch, you are telling customers a complete story about a business similar to theirs with similar problems, about the reasons that business decided to use your products or services to solve those problems, and about the tangible value it received from that decision. Suddenly you're not focused on you. It's about the customer.

As mentioned in the previous chapter, the listener, your sales opportunity, receives a lot of valuable information in the minute it takes you to tell the story:

- You are familiar with solving a problem such as theirs.

- Other companies have reviewed the alternatives and have chosen to work with you.

- You're providing your customers with a value-laden outcome.

When you tell sales stories, prospects get insights about their businesses as well as third-party validation of your product in less time than it takes an elevator to rise from the ground floor to the executive suite. Standard elevator pitches don't do that.

Networking and trade shows. Besides prospecting, sales stories do a great job of answering the "What do you do?" question in two other business development situations. First, networking events. If you are attending a conference or a networking event, you will meet someone and exchange cards. Then the person you met will look at your card and ask, "So, Kris, what is it that you do?" Answer with one of your sales stories. In fact, it is completely appropriate to ask that person what he does, so you can choose the right sales story to use. "Let me illustrate what we do with a 30-second story about one of my customers."

The second place where you frequently will hear the "What do you do?" question is at trade shows. A potential sales opportunity wandering the show floor stops by your booth. You are the first person to greet her. She looks at the signage in your booth and asks, "What do you guys do?" In trade shows, you have about 15 seconds to engage the interest of the buyer, so an elevator pitch about you and your founding history won't work. Instead, you would say, "Let me describe what we do with a brief story about one of our customers."

Discovery. Sales stories can be used to pose a question that will help clarify your understanding of a customer's requirements. Imagine that you have asked the customer a question about the problem that she is trying to solve. She gives you an answer, but you're not entirely certain that you understand it. An effective way to clarify a customer's requirements is to frame the problem within a story. "I want to be certain I understand your requirement. I have two customers who had similar sales problems to yours, and this is how they used our system to get sales back on track." Tell Story A and Story B and then ask, "Was Customer A or Customer B closer to your situation?"

It's like being in an optician's office for an eye exam with your face shoved into the phoropter (that mechanical device the optician uses to switch lenses back and forth to arrive at the right correction for you). The optician tests various combinations of lenses, flipping from one to another and asking, "Is this one better? . . . Or is this one better?" You can use sales stories to narrow down the prospect's priorities with a this-one-or-that-one approach.

Product presentation. At some point in every sales presentation, someone from the customer's side will ask, "How does your product do this?" or "How can we use your product to do this?" The typical default response is to describe the standard functions, features, and benefits of your product. You will have been trained not to dwell on the features but to talk about the benefits and value of your offering. The problem is that the customer is probably evaluating the products of multiple vendors, and it isn't easy to keep track of what one product does that another doesn't. Resorting to features-and-benefits statements places your message at risk of getting lost in the noise.

A better approach is to learn how to answer the how questions with a story. "Jack, that's a great question. Let me illustrate how we support this requirement. Larry B. is VP of marketing at GGG Industries, and he had a similar problem to solve." Suddenly you've switched from discussing the solution to the customer's problem in terms of your product to talking about why one or more existing customers selected your product and the tangible value they are receiving as a result.

Close of the sales cycle. You get a last-minute phone call from a prospective customer. You had hoped that he was calling to tell you that you won the order. Instead, you hear the last thing you wanted to hear: "We're almost there. We just a have a couple final questions we need answered." This can be a moment of dread. The call usually comes after you thought you were done. You believed that you had put all the customer's questions to bed. At this point, the biggest fear is that something will go wrong. You're concerned that nothing good can come from talking to the customer once all the questions have been answered. And you're doubly concerned because you believe that a competitor planted the questions in the customer's mind.

Use sales stories to answer these final questions. When a buyer is on the cusp of making a decision, a well-told story about why one of your current users selected and received value from your product can seal the deal. Final questions in a customer's decision-making process are more often about being reassured than about making the right decision. Some buyers are pioneers, and this third-party validation isn't important. However, many times purchasers are looking for substantiation and validation of their instincts. They want someone else to tell them that buying from you is a safe path to follow. A sales story can provide this assurance.

Asking for a referral. Sales stories are great tools to use when asking for referrals. In her book, *No More Cold Calling,* Joanne Black lays out a process for asking customers and other contacts for referrals. One of her rules is that you can't assume that your customers or contacts remember exactly what you do, which makes it hard for them to refer you to anyone. You have to remind them. This is a targeted use of a sales story. As in the last chapter, it's essential to make the story short and memorable. But just imagine how much stronger the referral will be if your contact can retell your sales story instead of the standard e-mail introduction.

Testimonials. Sales stories can be stronger than testimonials because they provide a complete tale. Testimonials tend to be snippets in praise of a job well done. But they leave out the backstory, the journey that led the customer to choose you in the first place. For someone who is looking to buy your product or service, it's not enough to know that you are doing a good job for your users. That prospective buyer wants to understand why your current customer made the decision to go with you. Your sales story will answer that (that's Question 3).

It's important to think about stories in a larger context. Sales stories are not only an educational tool, they are a way to inspire customers. Selling is a journey, and you need to move the customer to make the decision to join you. Success stories about similar customers will do that.

Sales stories are an effective way to create sales differentiation and stand out in the crowd. In Chapter 15, I showed the danger of your message being lost in the noise of a competitive sales situation. Sales stories will empower you to rise above the noise to be heard and remembered.

Sales stories simplify your selling. There is no simpler way to convey a value proposition than with a sales story. You're not explaining your value proposition in your terms. You're presenting it through the eyes of another customer. It demonstrates empathy for your buyer.

Sales stories resonate with satisficers. Remember that satisficers make the good-enough decision. They don't need to go the extra mile. Using sales stories to help a satisficer quickly understand how similar companies made their decisions to purchase from you can be very influential. It diminishes the need to invest additional time with other sellers.

Finally, a sales story well told can be a peak event or a peak experience in a customer's buying process. Regardless of whether the story is a peak event or the end contact, if it is memorable, it could be the winning moment for you.

PART VIII

Selling Through Customer Service

CHAPTER 38

Selling and Service

IN SALES, WE tend to categorize our customers as being in one of two states. They are in either a presale state or a postsale state. Salespeople have been conditioned to believe that responsibility for the customer shifts from sales to customer service once a customer gives you an order and moves from the presale state to the postsale state. Most of this book is focused on what salespeople should do during the traditional presale state.

As much as I have attempted to change your perceptions of what selling and buying are, I also want to change your perception of the role and responsibility of sales in servicing customers.

Let's start with the whole presale/postsale divide. I don't believe that a customer is ever in a postsales state. If managed appropriately, customers should be in a perpetual presales mode. After all, companies provide a high level of customer service not out of an altruistic sense of mission, but rather because they want to capture the customer's next order. And the one after that. And so on.

That's why when a customer calls your customer support group, it shouldn't be written off as a service call. Instead, every call to support should be considered a sales call for the customer's next order. How you, the salesperson, support a postsale customer will have a significant influence on the customer's next purchase.

Suddenly you are in the realm where actions speak louder than words. The nineteenth-century American essayist and poet Ralph Waldo Emerson provided words that should guide the actions of salespeople in servicing their customers: "What you do speaks so loudly I cannot hear what you say."

My first job in sales was with a major computer company whose CEO had the customer service philosophy that "We want to keep our customers surly, but not rebellious." True story. Our customers heard us loud and clear. I wish I could say that they limited themselves to being surly.

Sales made its own contribution to the mess. Long-held traditions in the sales bullpen dictated that phones were never answered after 4:55 P.M.—especially on Friday. It was bound to be a panicked customer whose system had crashed right when they were processing payroll checks for their employees. They needed assistance. Unfortunately, customer service turned off their phones even earlier on Friday.

All of which was just fine with the CEO. He felt that the solution to every problem was to sell the customer more computing equipment. Unsurprisingly, this did not prove to be a sustainable strategy.

That type of conscious disdain for your own customers has been thoroughly discredited. Few companies even attempt it. Even fewer do it and survive. The empowered customer of this Internet era holds most of the cards, and ferociously competitive markets force companies to compete on the basis of their customer service as well as their products.

What is the role of salespeople in providing customer service after the sale?

First, keep in mind that selling never stops. Even though customers' attention may be focused on implementation versus acquisition, they're counting on you to continue to provide additional insights about how to maximize the return on investment in your product.

It takes discipline to continue to curate and supply customers with valuable content after they place their order. In fact, you want to train your customers that communications from you deliver value. You want to maintain those Google alerts you established before getting the order. Send e-mails to customers with links to white papers and articles to let them know that you are continuing to think about their business and how you can be of service to them.

You'll have two distinct goals in these communications. First, you want to provide information that reinforces your customers' conviction that they made the right decision to purchase your product. Second, you want to begin to educate customers about what lies ahead of them in terms of the next purchase decision they'll have to make about your products. (A number of sales engagement tools make it easy for you to collect and store your content, communicate it to customers, and track their engagement with the content you provided.)

Another best practice for servicing customers is to publish a newsletter or other form of structured communication with your existing customers.

Remember that you are no longer just a salesperson. You are an expert. You are a trusted advisor. Your customers have invested in you once. However, that is not the end game. The end game is their continued investment in you. Now that you have set the bar by winning an order, how do you raise it to win the customer's next order? The answer is by working together to help the customer earn an even bigger return on her investment.

Two well-known account management strategies provide this service to customers. They provide distinct opportunities for you to help your customers earn a much bigger return on investment than they originally forecasted. One is called Fit In and Stand Out. The other is called Land and Expand.

Fit In and Stand Out. Dr. Seuss said, "Why fit in when you were born to stand out?" Fortunately, in sales it is not an either/or proposition.

You know that selling is about change. The change doesn't need to be big or transformative. Sometimes it's an incremental improvement for a particular customer function or process. For instance, assume that AXs, Inc. purchases your product to replace an existing and aging communication system. A condition of the sale requires that your product seamlessly integrate with AXs' existing processes and equipment. This integration is the Fit In part of the equation.

Once your product is successfully operational and delivering the value that you projected, you'll begin to educate the customer about how other companies have implemented your product to achieve even greater process improvements or cost savings. Help your customers realize a better return on the investment they have already made in your product by showing them how to use it more productively in order to generate incremental revenues, profits, or cost savings, and you will have provided a real service. That is the Stand Out part of the equation.

Land and Expand. Every customer has an ROI justification for purchasing your product. In this scenario, your task is to help the customer find additional uses of your product beyond the original business justification that will deliver incremental revenues and profits.

I worked for a company that sold a network connectivity product that replaced expensive telephone landlines. Part of our qualification criteria was that customers could realize a return on the full investment in the short term and had the longer-term potential to generate incremental return through the expanded use of our product.

We prospected for customers who could justify the entire cost of our system by replacing the most expensive 10 percent of their network sites (Land). Consequently, their incremental costs to replace the next most expensive 10 percent were substantially smaller. In this way, we could incrementally expand the usage of our product while continuing to reduce the unit cost to our customer (Expand).

The role of the salesperson in a Land and Expand service role is to find additional uses of your product for the customer beyond the original business case. Imagine your strategy as a target. Initially you will focus your efforts with the customer on the bull's-eye. When the opportunities in the bull's-eye are exhausted, then you shift your focus to the next ring out. And so on.

Remember, you are a trusted advisor to your customers. You've been proactive in helping them optimize their use of your product in order to achieve their business goals and maximize their ROI in your product. Your suggestions concerning how they can expand the uses of your product either to generate additional sales, increase margins by decreasing costs, or improve profitability by sharing the cost of your product among multiple cost centers are a real service.

CHAPTER 39

The Most Important Sales Call

ARE YOU SKIPPING the most important sales call of your sales cycle?

Salespeople routinely dig a hole and throw themselves in it after they close an order with a customer. You get an order, and your instinct is to quickly move on to the next prospect before the customer asks a question that you are afraid of answering out of fear that it will cause a change of mind.

Even though you have an order, you haven't finished the job of selling the customer. Your sales process doesn't stop with an order. There is one more very important step to take—one that can make the difference between a one-and-done and a long-term relationship with a loyal customer.

The most important sales call you make during the course of a sale is the first call *after* you receive their order and before the product is shipped or the service delivered.

Why?

To answer that question, let's examine a couple of immutable rules of what I call Andy Paul's Sales Calculus.

Sales Calculus rule 1. Your customers' expectations for your product or service expand logarithmically in proportion to the number of sellers that they talked to. This rule is pretty easy to understand. In competitive sales situations, customers are promised so many features, advantages, and benefits by so many different sellers that within 24 hours of making a decision, they have a hard time remembering which seller promised what. Instead, they have combined the best of what they heard and inflated it into a big fragile balloon of unreasonable expectations that is just waiting to pop.

Sales Calculus rule 2: For every degree of positive expectation on the part of the customer, there is a two-degree letdown when what you actually deliver doesn't precisely align with overinflated expectations. Having customers be unhappy with you because they believe that you overpromised and underdelivered, even though you give them just what they ordered, is not the ideal way to embark on a long-term relationship.

I see this happen with salespeople all the time. Fortunately, it is easily and completely avoidable.

Here are three tips to guide you in making this call:

Align the customer's expectations with your commitments. After you have received and accepted an order from your customer, pick up the phone and call the decision maker and/or the person who has responsibility for your product or service. Use your call notes, quotes, and proposals to summarize and walk the customer back through the buying process. Highlight the key requirements the customer had for the product purchased and review the commitments you made for how your product will meet or exceed those requirements. Review your proposal with the customer to make sure he precisely understands the products and features you contracted to deliver. The objectives of this important sales call are to reinforce the customer's own requirements in his mind, to refresh his memories about what he ordered (and why), and to clarify precisely what you are going to deliver and when. Your goal is to align the customer's expectations with your committed deliverables to ensure that his or her first perception of your product or service is positive.

Don't give in to your fears. The prevailing philosophy in many sales organizations is that the very last thing you should do is to call the customer immediately after you receive the order. Many sales managers and salespeople remain hostage to the irrational notion that you risk triggering a cancellation if you talk to the customer too soon after receiving an order. In my work, I have seen both sales managers and salespeople who believe that, although the customer may have given them the order, it was done only with great reluctance. Thus, they are afraid that if they speak with the customer after the order is received but before it is shipped, the customer will give in to some monstrous case of buyer's remorse that has been simmering just below the surface. I guess that could happen. But, in more than 30 years of selling, I have never witnessed it.

Make the call the first day after you receive the order. As previously stated, the most important sales call you make will be the first call to your customer after you receive an order. It's not a coincidence that it will also be the first sales call you make for the next order this customer will give you.

The Most Important Sales Call also plays a vital role in reducing, if not eliminating, buyer's remorse. People will tell you that buyer's remorse is a perfectly normal reaction on the part of your customers. I don't believe that.

According to a definition I found online, "Buyer's remorse is an emotional response on the part of a buyer in a sales transaction, which may involve feelings of regret, fear, depression, or anxiety."

Regret. Fear. Depression. Anxiety. These are not the emotions that we normally would associate with a long, healthy, and mutually profitable relationship with a customer. (Think of the upbeat testimonial you would get from a customer who experienced these emotions about buying from you: "Initially I was filled with self-loathing about my decision to buy from XYZ, Inc. But despite my anxieties about their product's abilities to meet our requirements, it hasn't been as bad as I feared.")

Buyer's remorse is a signal from your customer that the decision to purchase from you was perceived to be the least bad—or least risky—alternative. Risk is a trigger for fear, regret, and anxiety. When a customer chooses to buy from you, the decision maker may have a lot at stake from both a business and a personal standpoint. A buyer could fear that if your product or service doesn't perform as promised, it could negatively affect her career. A buyer's anxiety could also be based on the fear that a manager or peer inside the company will challenge the decision based on his or her perception of a better solution having been available.

To mitigate this perception of risk, you have to make it easy for the customer. You have to take the potential downsides from Sales Calculus rules 1 and 2 out of the equation by proactively making the Most Important Sales Call. It will have an immediate dampening effect on any incipient buyer's remorse the customer is developing. And it will continue to build the trust that is necessary for a long-term, productive relationship.

CHAPTER 40

Building Customer Relationships That Last

EFFECTIVE RELATIONSHIPS with customers are like my relationship with Riley, my Golden Retriever.

Like any good Golden Retriever, my buddy Riley is serenely uncomplicated and ecumenical with his affections. He loves anybody who plies him with kibble twice a day, patiently tosses him his ball, consents to be dragged along on the high-speed outings we still call walks, and tells him what a good boy he is.

The truth of the matter is that Riley doesn't really care who feeds and walks him. Anyone who makes him happy by completely taking care of his basic requirements earns his affections. That is all your customers want as well.

A productive and lasting relationship with a customer is all about needs and deeds. Customers have needs. And their relationship with you extends only to the degree that you meet and exceed those needs with your deeds.

Like our canine companions, customers have developed a simple hierarchy of needs: Give me timely, complete, and accurate information to make an informed purchase decision; live up to your promises and deliver on your commitments; and, most important, support me without condition.

And, just like Riley, customers don't care who meets their needs. It could be you. Or it could be the sales rep from your prime competitor. Customers may like you, but they don't care about you. Customers care only about what you have done and can do for them.

If you aren't there to meet their needs, customers will quickly forget that you exist. Who has ever had to leave a beloved dog to go off to college or move away from home? You know your dog loves you absolutely and completely, until the car taking you to the airport disappears around the corner. At which point, they will have largely forgotten about you and bonded with the new person supplying the kibble and the walks. Your customers are the same way.

Here are three strategies to build lasting needs-and-deeds relationships with your customers.

Practice equivalence. The principle that all salespeople should be guided by in servicing their customers is what I call "equivalence." The Golden Rule—which we all learned in childhood—states that you should treat others the way you would want them to treat you. That is what equivalence means in selling and service.

Ask yourself: If you were a customer of your own company, what would you expect the customer experience to be? How would you wish to be treated by your own sales and support people? That should be the minimum standard of care that you provide to your own prospects and customers. This is easy to start with but requires constant attention.

One of my CEO clients was a very demanding consumer. That was his right. However, it was often stressful to go to restaurants with him because he demanded perfection in the food and service and was not bashful about sending dishes back to the kitchen. Yet, when it came to his own customers, he was defensive about his products and adopted a minimalist approach to customer service, making it a challenge for customers to get the support they needed. It took a long time to help him recognize and acknowledge the inconsistency between the service he expected when he purchased a product and the way he treated his own customers. Only then did he start earning the repeat business he needed to really grow his company.

Much like the other strategies in this book, you can practice equivalence even if your company doesn't embrace it. The actions you can take to demonstrate a higher level of support are under your control.

You have to constantly survey yourself about how well you are doing with these tasks and other basic sales responsibilities. Are you promptly returning calls? Are you meeting the expectations you set with customers? It's easy to let your guard down. But your customer's time is every bit as important as yours. Every time you have the opportunity to interact with your customer, be absolutely certain that you are providing a level of service that is no less than what you would be satisfied to receive if you were the customer.

Delight your customers with your commitment to customer service. Commit to being completely responsive to your customers' requirements for support, both presale and postsale. The first step to take internally is to eliminate the distinction in your mind between presale and postsale support. All support is presale. As soon as a customer gives you an order, all of your support should be provided with the goals of having a satisfied customer who will give you the next order and receiving a great referral to another potential customer.

Another of my clients had a simple escalation procedure in place: All calls to sales and service were to be answered by a live person. If the front-line sales or service tech were not available, the call was bumped to a manager. If the manager was busy, the call was routed to a VP and then up to the CEO. The CEO routinely answered calls from customers. He never identified himself to customers by other than his first name when he helped them. Imagine how powerful it was for customers to learn later that the CEO had so humbly helped them.

Demonstrate your appreciation for the opportunity to serve your customers. With Riley this is as easy as scratching his back and telling him, "Good boy." Customers may not welcome the physical contact, but they always like to hear that you appreciate the opportunity to earn their business.

You'll notice I didn't say that customers like to hear that you appreciate their business. I'm sure they do. But I learned a lesson a long time ago that what they really want to hear is that you are going to work hard every day to continue to earn the right to win their business. Demonstrate by your words and deeds that there is no danger of your becoming complacent and taking the customer for granted. The strategies I covered in the previous chapter, those to help your customers maximize their return on their investment in your product, demonstrate your appreciation for the opportunity to work with them and to earn their trust and confidence in return.

Finally, it is important to be consistent. I had a CEO client, Dan, who complained to me one day about a frustrating experience trying to get customer service from a camera company. He had gone on their website to find a customer service number to call. There wasn't one. Just a form to fill in and submit. He didn't want to do that. He wanted to talk to someone. So he called the main number for the company, which was listed on the website. Dan described to me how he became more and more worked up as he navigated the auto-attendant and began to realize that the company didn't have an extension for customer service. After ten minutes, he hung up in frustration. I said to him that he must really hate auto-attendants. He said he certainly did. I asked if he thought that auto-attendants were a good customer service tool. Dan emphatically disagreed. I picked up my phone, dialed it, and handed it to him. I asked him, "Then why do you use it in your business?"

Practice equivalence at all times. And keep an eye out for the small inconsistencies in your processes that can send a damaging message that you don't intend.

Index